MARTIN
GRUPI

HELLO FLOWER

A REAL LIFE STORY
OF NARCISSISTIC LOVE
AND INVISIBLE ABUSE

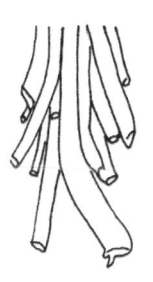

Copyright © 2024 Martina Gruppo

Book design by Paul-Hawkins.com
Artwork © 2024 Linn Hart
Cover by Paul Hawkins and Linn Hart

All rights reserved. No part of this book may be reproduced or used in any manner without written permission of the copyright owner except for the use of quotations in a book review. This book is a memoir reflecting *my* recollections and experiences, some dialogue may have been recreated but words tend to stick and I have recounted them here to the best of my ability. Some names and characteristics have been changed and some events compressed. Memory is subjective, therefore names and places may have been changed or entirely omitted.

First edition 2024

ISBN: 9798325952456
Also available as an eBook

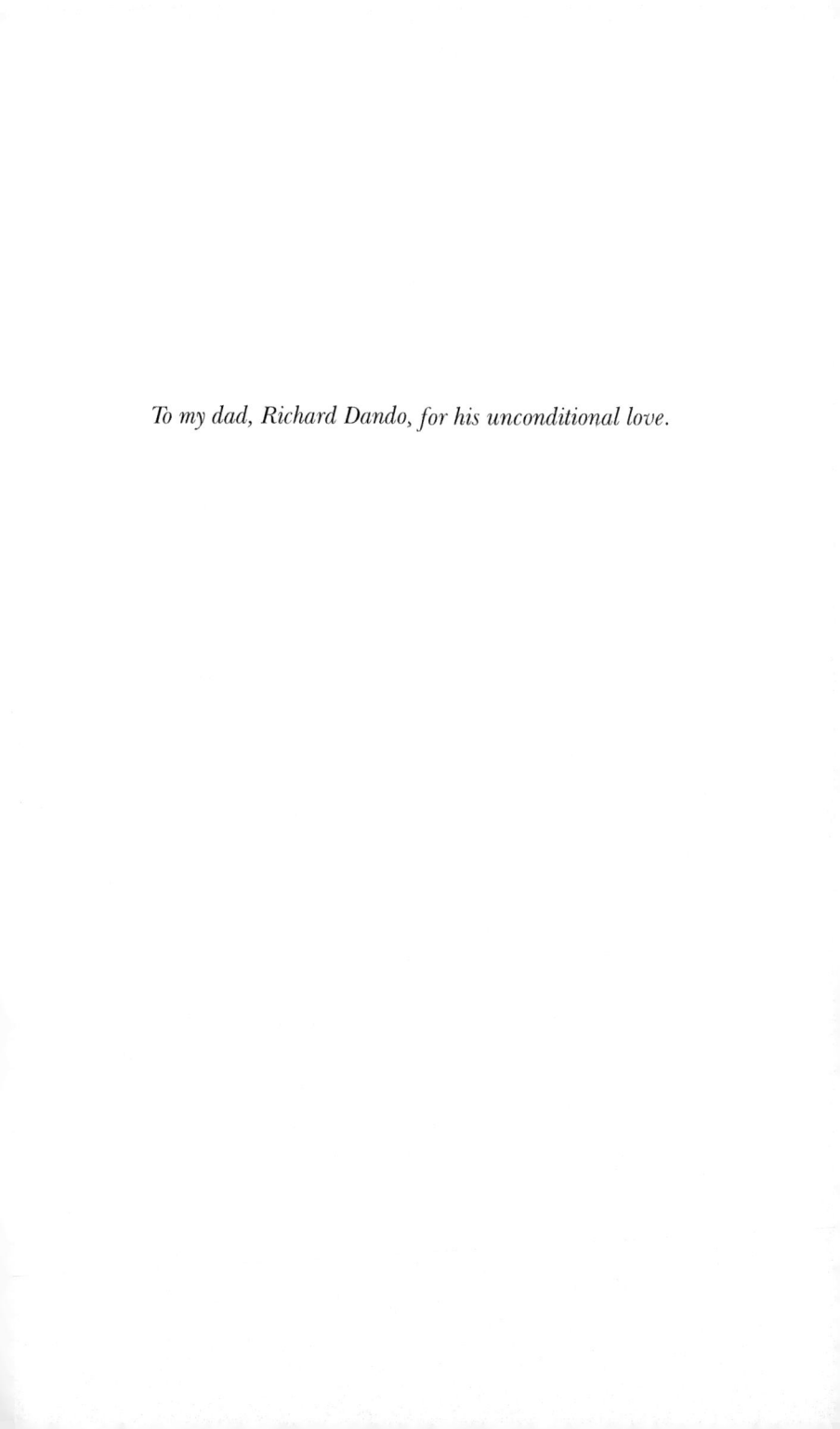

To my dad, Richard Dando, for his unconditional love.

Prologue

February 2022

The house was dirty and dusty with unfinished work and various tools left lying around. One bedroom contained a new bed and mattress, while my belongings remained unpacked in boxes.

The newly fitted front door was locked, and there was a padlock on the gate, just in case.

Looking out at the wintry garden full of bare fruit trees, my gaze followed the old broken brickwork which made half-hearted attempts to hide the uneven footpath. I sighed deeply.

Curious to know what was holding my attention, my dog lolloped over to my side and stared through the glass but finding nothing of interest went back to his cushion placed perfectly on the concrete floor and stretched out groaning contentedly in a patch of sunlight.

Smiling at him, I turned back to look at the garden, and a flash of pale yellow caught my eye. A row of flowers I had never noticed before had sprung up, right in the middle of the patchy grass.

Narcissi.

'Hello Flower,' I whispered.

Chapter 1

Be careful what you wish for

It was March 2011, and I was on my way to Gatwick airport. With tense knuckles on the steering wheel, I found it hard to navigate the numerous roundabouts while concentrating on the directions coming out of the satnav. The device's crisp clear tones wasn't the only voice I was listening to.

On BBC Radio 2, Jeremy Vine was talking about how many people were returning to their first love after decades apart, reuniting with the person they fell hopelessly in love with in their teens or early twenties. 'Has this happened to you?' he asked. '*Me!*' I screamed joyfully at the radio. '*It is happening right now to ME.*' I wanted to call the radio. I wanted to share the most romantic story I believed they would ever broadcast, but no matter how much my fingers were itching to dial the number and call in, I couldn't; I didn't have time to share my utter joy.

Instead, I pelted down the A272, tense with butterflies, anticipation, and pure, genuine, unadulterated love. I had a plane to catch and a piece of missing history to rewrite. I was on my way to Rome to meet up with the one person I had loved more than life itself nearly twenty years previously. This wasn't a whim or a quick bunk-up; this was *the* person I was always supposed to have been with—*The One*. Had I known then what the next ten years would bring, I would have double-backed at the next roundabout and hightailed it home.

Bloody, bloody hindsight, always late to the party.

This would be my once-upon-a-time, the fairytale we all dream of. The gorgeous, laid-back Prince Charming who had been mine, and then he wasn't, had once again come charging back into my life as I had always hoped but never expected.

Initially, we fall for the love or the 'feels' as the younger lot would probably call it. That head-over-heels-sure feeling that they are the right one for you. That original love story everyone craves you know the one – a *'set in the stars destiny' 'meant to be'* tale of romantic, heart-stoppingly beautiful love. The kind where you forget to eat and moon around, behaving like a total moron only prettier, sparklier, ditzier, but you can forgive yourself because you have found your soulmate.

We want all that romance with a dose of reality to bring the happy pink heart-shaped balloon back down to earth again and maybe even deflate or burst. Then we root for it to be mended and float merrily on its way. We are addicted and gripped by films, TV series and even real-life stories where hard-won love plays out, cheering for the hero or heroine to overcome all the obstacles life places in their path just so we can bask in their deeper, more meaningful, happy-ever-after.

Of course, there are ups and downs; we expect them because that is the structure on which strength and endurance are built. All solid relationships and friendships are like that. It takes work, compromise, more work and then you can feel the benefits of something grounded in firm foundations. Everything else rests on the hope that the other person will want to meet you in the middle, will want what is best for you, will want that you work together for a lovely future, having each other's back. It helps if you have a great rapport with family members, friends, and even work colleagues, but on paring it back, the bottom line is it's just the two of you, so you want to make sure they are the right one.

This is all well and good if you are both on that same track, but while there may be a general belief that love changes everything, I'm afraid I have disappointing news for you— it doesn't. Sadly, I can say that with some authority.

My misguided notion of a healthy, happy relationship was based on the notion that whatever happened, you could always rely on the other person. It was less about money or where or how you lived and more about caring how your better (or worse?) half felt. Doing whatever you could to make them happy, no matter how small, silly or ridiculous, your role was to make the other person feel special with whatever means available. They become your priority, not excluding all others, but in the general shopping list of life, they are pretty much at the top: considered, prioritised and unique to you.

Unfortunately, nothing in this world can prepare you for the utter loneliness and misery of fighting to save a marriage all by yourself.

Parasitical
OF, OR PERTAINING TO, HAVING THE CHARACTERISTICS OF A PARASITE; LEECHLIKE OR FREELOADING.

I used to say that I knew what true love was because if he was in one room and I was in the other, I would miss him. Now, sadly, I couldn't pick out love from a heart-shaped lineup, but I am all too familiar with loneliness and can recognise it in a relationship. It's the same as wearing an invisibility cloak – it doesn't matter what you do, say, how you dress, or how hard you try – you simply aren't there.

You don't matter.

This isn't the story I wanted or expected to write, but it needs to be told, to help me work through something I still cannot believe I allowed to happen, especially to someone like me.

Chapter 2

Me

At nineteen years of age, I was considered a bit of a handful. It was nothing criminal, but I had been asked to leave my sixth-form college in the South West of England because of the effect my disturbing and negatively influential behaviour had on the rest of the Theology class. I was allowed back for exams as my English language and literature tutor felt I had potential.

Frankly, I had lost interest in formal education. I knew what I wanted to do: travel and learn new languages. I liked the idea of working with children, so I planned to live in several European capital cities long enough to hold my own in the language, and once I was fluent in two or three, I intended to return to the UK, open an international creche and have a large family. The End.

As a career trajectory, it didn't exactly meet adult approval. My parents made it very clear if that was my plan, I would need to finance it myself until my inevitable failure and subsequent return to England to find a 'real' job.

How do you solve a problem like Martina? Feisty, stubborn, cheeky. I wasn't a pushover, but I was a people pleaser. In retrospect, they make a good combination, depending on who needs to be pleased and how far they are willing to push. Not one none of my friends could understand why I was so determined to leave, living abroad was such an extreme move. Somehow it made sense to me despite having a long-term relationship with an older, rich, abusive boyfriend.

He didn't mean to hit me; he had never hit anyone else before. Must be me then.

He ran a successful business and was having my engagement ring made. To pay for it, he needed to sell his Rolex. *That's* how much he loved me. I had 'designed' the ring. I was nineteen years old, so in an act of rebellion, I requested a square shape with sapphires because I like the colour blue. I cannot remember him ever asking to marry me, but it was almost a done deal. We would be married after I had spent twelve months in France learning the language, and then I would return. He said he understood why I wanted to do this, but he continued to lose his temper.

It started with a slap, but the more I took and the less I gave back (I did retaliate a couple of times, much to his astonishment), the more violent he became. In the end, I just took it because it was easier. I felt this was down to me. My parents hated him, which felt like a failing on my part, so I mainly put up with it. Eventually, though, even I had my 'tipping point'. I can't quite remember when that was. I don't think it was when he cracked a couple of my ribs one Sunday after I had been chatting on the phone for too long. Or that time in the street in the middle of the day, when I was teasingly not giving him a piece of fudge from the packet I had bought, his hands were full carrying his coat and briefcase, so he headbutted me.

The more I think about it, I'm pretty sure it was the time we went on holiday to Turkey, and he punched me on the nose late at night because I had wanted to stay dancing in a restaurant. As I was trying to stem the blood flow from my nose with the bed sheets and next door were banging on the wall because of the shouting, he was busy packing everything up in his case and dividing the passports while at the same time telling me he was leaving because I was unable to behave. He left the room, and I sat there preoccupied with how to clean up the blood. I was probably in shock as I didn't move and was still sitting in the same position when he returned, this time to tell me how heartbroken he was that I hadn't followed him.

Yes, I believe that was the last time I allowed it. Every time, he swore it was entirely out of character and promised it would never happen again—until it did. Something about that last time was so horrific even he knew he had crossed a line. I made it very clear I would never accept any physical violence again. I didn't exactly finish it with him; I was, however, very much done with being his punchbag, and, for once, he didn't argue with me.

I couldn't take the job in France. They needed someone who could ski, or maybe the timings were slightly out. However, it wasn't an issue. The family had a friend in Rome who needed a mother-tongue English nanny, and this time, they were paying for my ticket over there. I couldn't pack quickly enough.

He assured me he would visit with the ring.

* * *

I truly believe many of us fall in love with one capital city in our lifetimes. We may find others pretty, beautiful or unique, but whether abroad or at home our hearts belong to just one.

Rome unexpectedly stole my heart.

It happened as the taxi drove from the airport to the centre of the city. Nervous and excited, I stared out the window, and my heart turned somersaults. It was stunning! The grandeur, the buildings, the river, the streets, everything from the sense of history to the stylish Italians walking along the pavements, I fell head over heels before I even stepped out of the taxi.

My excitement was short-lived. The new job: awful people, dreadful. Their idea was to pay as little as possible while expecting me to be a nanny, language teacher, maid, cleaner and cook for their two children. From 7 a.m. till I fell into bed exhausted at 10 p.m. once all the ironing was complete. This I was to do for five and a half full days a week. '*You have Sundays off*' I was told, as if this was some reluctant extra they were indulging me in.

I quickly made friends with other nannies and babysitters and soon formulated an escape plan: I would put up with their terms and conditions, spoilt kids and dreadful pay only for as long as it took to find a better job. Giving up and going home was never an option.

Italy was an eye-opener, and I felt at home, but the attention I received was unlike anything I had ever experienced before. I had always considered myself a bit too much—too tall, too thin, eyes too slanty, lips too big. I never quite fit in, yet here I was, no longer the square peg round hole with a gobby attitude type. Suddenly, I was being noticed, and not by scrawny-looking older men with too much money and pent-up aggression. Instead, the attention came from a very attractive-looking set of blokes with smiling eyes and smooth chat-up lines unmistakably directed at me. Looking different was no longer a disadvantage but quite the opposite. I couldn't believe it, but that's not to say I didn't welcome it.

Who wouldn't?

I felt comfortable and totally at ease; Italy felt like somewhere I belonged. I loved the language and learnt it quickly. When I was very young we spent summers in the north of Italy visiting friends and family. I seemed to have an ear for languages, and by listening closely, I honed my language skills. I am also nosy and curious, and I wanted to understand what others were saying and be involved, so I copied the accent, pretended I could understand when I couldn't and listened intently. Within a few months I became pretty fluent.

I credit Rome with making me realise that being with someone who uses their fists to make their point is not a life choice. I was genuinely happy in that city. I was having proper fun, and tellingly, I never cried; I wasn't miserable, at all, quite the change from my life back in Blighty.

I started to see someone, and although he probably had another girlfriend tucked away, it was easy and fun and not terribly serious. On one occasion he turned around to talk to me when I was in the back of the car. I flinched and ducked, convinced he was going to hit me. His shocked expression told me everything.

So, when ol' Fisticuffs turned up in Italy with the ring and a marriage proposal, I knew what I had to do. I briefly visited him in his hotel and very politely told him no, I was not up for a life of misery, endless crying and bruises. Thanks, but no thanks. It wasn't pleasant, but I was a different person; I knew it and he could see it. He went back to the UK and told everyone in my home town how much I had changed and how broken he was. Which was rich, considering how many times he had actually broken me. I put them right when I, too, returned a month or so later for a short visit, no longer needing to cover up his physical abuse from various friends. I made sure they knew exactly why I didn't fancy a lifetime of him and why six months of happiness and no more tears in Rome had shown me exactly where I wanted to be.

I didn't stay for long on that trip home, much to the shock of my family, who had been laying bets on how quickly I would be back for good. I made it clear to everyone that I was doing fantastically well, and I had no idea for how long or what I would end up doing, but it felt right. It was interesting how many people told me how *luc*ky I was living in Italy. Luck had nothing to do with it, I hadn't even paid for my flight out there. I didn't want to work in a high-end shoe shop or carry on studying, I wanted to burst into my twenties having fun and seeing the world. It didn't make it a better or worse choice; it made it *my* choice.

I adored the weather, the food, the unexpected attention and the general way of life. It was the late 80s, and Rome felt like it belonged to us. Everyone knew someone who knew someone. The places we went to were few and popular, and we knew exactly who the regulars were at each one and when the best nights were. These *locale* pubs, bars and privately owned drinking spots, many of which turned into underground clubs at the weekend, were scattered around the city centre. Nothing commercial existed. The restaurants were owned by generations of families, the bars had people who had worked there for years, Airbnb was unheard of, and the hotels were huge, expensive and old-fashioned.

There were only a couple of larger supermarkets; the rest were family-owned *alimentaris* (grocery shops). Fast food was a slice of pizza or *suppli* (a small deep fried ball of risotto with mozzarella set deliciously in the middle) to keep you going till the regular mealtime. It wasn't sanitised or set up for tourists; they were the visitors and had to adapt to how Rome was back then. The city belonged to the people who lived there, and we felt part of it. Whether we were there as a nanny or working in offices, there was no hierarchy; if there was, it didn't touch us. This was our city and we adored it.

It was 1989, and I was having a lot of fun. I wasn't looking for true love, but then isn't that always the way?

Chapter 3

Found You

I spent the first couple of years in Rome living the dream, I suppose. I wasn't particularly well behaved, and it was utterly glorious. My main responsibility was keeping down a well-paid job as a nanny, which I did, admirably, considering the late nights, excessive consumption of alcohol and the rest. We all knew so many people and new arrivals were welcomed and introduced. We made pasta dinners for groups of up to a dozen, and then, after food, we were all off out somewhere in the city till the early hours to some pub or club. Our group of international, hard-working, hard-drinking, giggling, laughing reprobates were truly welcome everywhere in that magical city.

It was the best time of my life.

Eventually, I stopped working as a nanny and found employment in a pub that turned into a club on the weekends—very much illegally, but that all added to the fun. I had my own place in the centre close to where I worked, and things were pretty much OK. I was still making serious mistakes in terms of relationships—an affair with a married man seemed like a good idea for a while, but it wasn't making for a happy union.

When out for dinner one night, I was choosing a second course, and when I asked what he would be having for seconds, he looked at me and said '*You*' and smiled. I fired back that I was sick of always being second, and as I said it, I realised how true that was. I didn't want another older, messed-up man. He may not have been handy with his fists, but was that all I deserved? A philandering short arse not quite old enough to be my father (but close) and a few nights out a week to some fancy restaurant where he figured he wouldn't be recognised.

I ended it.

The bar/pub/club I worked in was the perfect distraction. It was popular with foreign nannies and the locals who loved to chat them up. It was while I was working there that I first noticed him. It was 1992.

* * *

When I was about six years old, my brother had a pair of jeans with the cowboy character Lucky Luke printed on the flare at the bottom. I can still see that picture. I studied it and fell in love with it for reasons I cannot even begin to explain: the carefree attitude, the couldn't-careless slouch, the sleepy gaze and even the cigarette hanging off his perfect lips. I didn't realise it at that age, but this image imprinted on my brain was my dream man, and it sat waiting patiently in my subconscious until presenting itself to me in life form in a bar in Italy.

Tall Italians stand out. It's a fact, I am not being sizeist. Generally speaking, they are not the leggiest race in the world, but he certainly was. I clocked his mates first, all shapes and sizes, flashy smiles, confident swagger, chat-up lines and cocky attitudes, and then him.

Lanky, tall, never-ending legs, melting brown eyes, a shy smile and the blackest hair with a shock of white at the front. The most beautiful thing I had ever seen. I studied him slyly, feigning disinterest. No way was I going to let him know *how I felt*. From the way he threw furtive glances my way, it seemed I wasn't the only interested party. It went on like that for a while, no one doing anything, but it felt exciting, like a ticking bomb.

He told my work colleagues he had spotted me in another club a few months previously and had fallen for me then but had been too shy to approach me. He was borderline obsessed, he told them, and had been intent on finding me. He didn't tell me any of this. Instead, he fed the information, then sat back and waited for it to be passed on. Which it was, of course. Everyone loves a love story.

My initial, and I am proud to say sceptical, reaction had been, '*Which club?*' The honest reaction of someone who would definitely have noticed her fantasy boyfriend come to life if they really had been in the same place at the same time. The excitement of those messengers brushed off my suspicions, '*It was so romantic, so beautiful,*' they said. '*Meant to be.*' All that damned crap that people pile on when they want a hand in creating someone's Happy Ever After.

I believed it because I wanted it too. Someone my age, tick, tall, tick, gentle, tick, has a girlfriend... oh, just a minor issue, that one. I remember being told by the Happy Ever After crew (who were growing in numbers every day) that he wasn't that into her, that they were having problems and that he was trying to extricate himself from a delicate situation.

'Delicate' is an understatement. I was told afterwards that she had attempted suicide. He assured me that he had been trying to end it for a while as she was not stable. Her friends hated me and blamed me as the wicked foreign girl. His friends blamed her. Guess who no one blamed?

He told me, with a sombre face, that he had tried telling her again and again it simply wasn't working. She apparently wouldn't listen, wouldn't accept it, and he was at his wit's end trying to be as gentle as possible. I really felt for him. Poor bloke trying desperately to do the right thing, be honest and kind, yet there was precious little he could do in the face of such madness. He just wanted to be free to love me because I was definitely '*the one*'. He told me he had imagined me exactly as I was, with almond-shaped eyes and long legs. He wasn't keen on Italian girls and had always been attracted to foreigners. As it seemed to mirror everything I felt, I believed every word. Of course, I felt bad for his ex-girlfriend, but he explained sadly that she really was unhinged.

I wasn't sure I felt great about the fact that all the girls in that particular circle hated me, I was an outsider—fine working the bar, but taking one of theirs? That was not on. He shrugged it off and said they'd all get over it in time, convincing me they were simply envious and only we mattered. His band of brothers, however, loved the drama and the whole mess of the situation. They all courted the idea of a fun, exotic, foreign girlfriend, someone independent instead of a clingy Italian girl looking to settle down, and he had given them hope.

I had found the love of my life, nothing and nobody could persuade me otherwise. Someone once said, '*Love feels like there is nothing you can do about it.*' Yes, that was exactly it—nothing at all to be done.

Like all idiots of that age, I knew what was best for me.

Chapter 4

Dreams don't work unless you do

We led an idyllic life. I held down three jobs: bar work, teaching, and live-out part-time nannying. Money was more than OK. Life in Rome was a social whirl of parties, clubs, eating out, and having the best time ever.

He didn't seem to be working, but that made it much easier if I needed to be picked up or taken to and from work. It was ideal, a gorgeous boyfriend always on hand to take me wherever I needed to go. He had the car, and while I was busy at work, he was at the gym his friend owned, which I also attended for free, thanks to him. Or he was off organising some catwalk show with a friend of his who wanted me to wear their designs as a favour, and when they paid a load of money, he just smiled happily at me, so proud it had worked out for us.

We had a remarkable lifestyle. As a result of being considered a transient foreigner, I found us an economical apartment in a really expensive part of the city; luckily for me a friend of his wanted to share it too, so he came to live with us. Very soon lots of people would just turn up at all hours of the day and night and hang out at ours. It was hedonistic and fun but also tiring at times because I was often working till the early hours, and sometimes the idea of half a dozen of his mates gathered in my tiny kitchen cooking pasta and smoking endless joints at three in the morning didn't always appeal. He would take great care of me and ask them to leave in hushed tones as he explained I had requested some peace.

I was living a great life, busy with plenty of work to cover food and rent. I had an incredible, charming, and popular boyfriend whom everyone said was obsessed with me. He was evidently adored by all who knew him. I was the lucky one. As in all fairytales, reality eventually bites, and very soon, my Prince Charming's group of reliable party friends were now looking for long-term job opportunities or creating stable relationships and establishing financial security through the property market. They were looking at their futures and planning for it. I loved our lifestyle but was bright enough to know that it wasn't sustainable. I was certainly working hard, making more than enough money to keep us both, but ultimately, I started questioning where we were going. What was going to happen to us.

What was *our* plan for *our* future?

He dismissed any planning possibility out of hand. '*So boring,*' he would moan. '*Life was to be lived in the moment*' and '*Why couldn't we just carry on as we are?*' He wasn't interested in settling down, whatever that entailed. He wanted nothing to change. He smiled and continued to do his bit in our day-to-day lives by sticking sweet love notes for me to find on the bathroom mirror. No change is all well and good when the sun is shining, the days are endless, and you are one half of a deliciously good-looking and loved up couple, invited everywhere and to everything by everyone. However, I had a nagging feeling because for all that this life was great and fun, I just couldn't imagine it long term. Nor did I want to. I wasn't stupid. I may have been in love, and I certainly idolised him, but I wanted so much more for us. I knew we couldn't keep this going; pulling all-nighters and finding extra piecemeal work to supplement my earnings was losing its shine. I was in my mid-twenties, and it was time to change gear.

Italy was great for food, weather, Vespas, sharp clothes and relaxed attitudes towards pretty much everything, but career options in the early 90s were slim pickings. The possibility of starting, let alone advancing a career, was convoluted, to say the least. For any permanent work contract, you had to know someone or have some tenuous connection to a member of their family. It didn't matter if they had no idea who you were as long as someone along the line had some vague connection to you. Then and only then could you be recommended.

Jobs were certainly available for foreigners, but were always temporary, short-term and usually cash-in-hand. Nanny/babysitting positions were abundant and pitifully paid, but with the pre-requisite that you spoke mother-tongue English and passable Italian—we wouldn't want to confuse the children. Beggars can't be choosers, but if a parent can have someone double up and use a private tutor as a skivvy, then they will choose that option every single time.

I tried applying for a more serious type of office vacancy, so desperate was I to stay in Italy and 'further myself', but fluent Italian and English mother tongue weren't enough. Another language and a degree were needed.

I didn't necessarily want to 'grow up', but I did want to be able to decide what to do next. To do that, my skills needed to exceed fluent Italian, cocktail-making and being great with kids. England was calling me. That was where the opportunities for both of us to succeed lay. I wasn't exactly sure at what, but I just assumed we would figure it out together.

I was ready for the next stage. I thought he was too.

I had *the* conversation with him—the one your parents have with you about your future, when they try to pin you down about maybe growing up a little, taking responsibility, choosing your life path. Or at least I tried to. I asked what exactly he wanted to do. He sat there chewing his lip, mulling it over as if it had never occurred to him. He wasn't sure, maybe something in fashion, although how he would go about it was a mystery.

He certainly knew what he *wasn't* prepared to do. His exclusion list of jobs covered any sort of training, all types of further education and any kind of menial job as a starting point. I tried to be understanding. I wasn't keen on further education and hated exams. Everyone had their thing; we just needed to find his. I listened to his musings, and, in my head, I justified it all. I would help him find whatever his dream was. We were, after all, a couple and in this together. I was still mulling over the idea of returning to England, and I threw open the idea of him coming with me to learn English as I believed that would be a massive help in his 'ambition' to work in fashion. I told him there were so many opportunities over there, but he was unimpressed, citing the cold, damp, inconsistent weather as a deterrent, not to mention the unappetising food. I thought he was joking.

If hindsight is merely wishful thinking, but time travel becomes available, then I plan on returning and giving my naive 24-year-old self a really hard slap to wake me up from that fog of stupidity.

I felt very differently. It would be hard to change things, and I wasn't that sure what I wanted to do or be and certainly no one was sitting me down to have that same conversation, not him or anyone from my family.

Somewhere inside me, I knew I needed to attain a degree (my Irish mother had drilled that into me from the moment I could speak). I knew, too, that until I had one, I wouldn't have a choice in what I did next, and as a fairly strong- willed and focused young woman, choices were fundamental to me.

Unfortunately, I was on my own with my big ideas of cementing our lives and futures together because any changes, especially one involving an international move, were out of the question for him. Admittedly, he didn't ever agree to us breaking up, and he was willing to do anything for love, anything to keep us together, anything except *that*. The more determined I was to make a move to further my career, the more relaxed he seemed about me pursuing a life away from him. '*Of course, I love you,*' he assured me. But not enough apparently to take the next step, and although it would be difficult, he wasn't interested in the idea of moving to the UK as he didn't know the language or the people. He adored his own country and wanted to stay and carve his future there as I did in my home country. He was prepared to let me go despite it being such a shame. I mean, we were so good together, he claimed, but I seemed set on going back, and he didn't want to be the one to stop me from doing what I wanted.

I felt he was behaving altruistically, allowing me to leave. He understood why I needed to go. He wasn't happy about it, but he loved me so much and respected my reasons for going: '*Your choice,*' he told me, as he didn't want to pressure me either way. Of course he would visit, and I could go back at any time, and we would be together again.

It all sounded possible. We could do this. It would be hard, but I was convinced we were strong enough to make it work, a short-term separation for our amazing future. I was heartbroken, optimistic and hopeful.

Pollyanna would have been proud.

Chapter 5

Head 1 - Heart 0

Six years feels like a lifetime in your twenties, but six years abroad feels like a lifetime on another planet. I was back 'home', and I could not have felt more out of place —a foreigner in my own country. It was 1994, and it felt cold, unwelcome and unfamiliar.

Despite my absolute belief that this was the right thing to do, being back home somehow felt uncomfortable. People were naturally getting on with their lives and had been quite happily progressing without me. They made sure I was under no illusion they needed to hear anything about who, where, what or how things had been in that unfamiliar place I had spent some pretty formative years. It's interesting how uninterested people can be. The only question they managed was whether I had seen the Pope. Coming from an Irish Catholic family, I guess that was only to be expected.

I managed to disappoint them on that front too.

Desperate to shake off the image of a travelling loser and prove to everyone that I hadn't just binned my most important further educational years, I was accepted on a BA Hons course through clearing at a North London Polytechnic. Relief all round, I was welcomed back into the fold, suddenly not entirely the waster dropout they had expected. Maybe there was hope.

I enrolled as a mature student, and I certainly felt ancient at twenty-six years old. I stood out like a sore thumb, from my clothes to my opinions, my taste in food, and my retro music preferences. Unlike the teenagers in my first house-share who draped themselves over various pieces of furniture, weeping periodically over the breakup of Take That, I could not have cared less.

A fish out of water was an understatement. I had an awful lot of re-adjusting to do. I missed being in Italy: the weather, the food, the people and especially speaking the language. I became tongue-tied searching for the correct words in my own language, whereas I had a million Italian phrases I could have instantly used to express myself, hand gestures too, but they just made me more of an oddity, so I learnt to keep my arms still. I stared too much and for too long without realising, yet another bad habit I needed to stop. English people don't stare; it isn't the 'done thing' unless you plan on starting a fight. It was all so different, but gradually, I adapted and learned to cope and understand what was and wasn't acceptable.

The empty feeling I carried inside wasn't going to adjust as easily.

I missed my old life, the freedom, the late nights and later mornings, the lack of responsibility, the chaotic volume and the people, and the man I had left behind. I missed him and everything about him. Talking was expensive and infrequent. He didn't call as it was 'difficult', so I called whenever I could. He sounded sad but claimed he hated talking on the phone as it wasn't the same, and I couldn't blame him. Mobile phones were relatively new, although technology was everywhere if you were brave enough to use it. I was convinced it was a passing phase and was shocked the computer classes at the North London campus were compulsory and terrifying – then again, fax machines, which had been around for a while, were nothing short of a miracle as far as I was concerned – but the brain is a clever old organ, it grows and absorbs and learns how to deal with whatever is thrown at it.

The heart, on the other hand, has a much harder time accepting change.

I had no interest in snakebite and black at the student bar, and I wasn't even convinced I was on the right course; French, yes, I had a purpose for that, European Economics less so. Had I totally messed up by leaving the city I had called home for six years and the one person I was sure was my soulmate? I had to fly back, to make sure that everything I believed in was still there, and as soon as my student loan made an appearance, I used it for something far more essential than food or textbooks. I booked a flight. I needed to be with him, just as much as I was sure he needed to be with me.

I have a photo of us during that visit. It is pitiful. I look desperate and clingy; my smile doesn't reach my eyes because my expression is anxious and strained. My face is set so tightly I could have lockjaw.

When I see those photos, my heart hurts for the hopeful young woman I was. My excitement at seeing him again and being reunited is something I have cancelled out. Looking at that picture, I can see the dictionary definition of utter desolation. He, on the other hand, could not look more chilled, giving off the vibe of someone so totally comfortable in his own skin he could be on holiday. Unconcerned and laid back, just another convivial weekend, one girl briefly swapped out for the old one who was back in town. I wasn't aware of that then, or maybe, on reflection, I did suspect something. But I was surrounded by a familiar bunch of his friends, laughing, joking, welcoming, and entirely complicit in his secret.

One evening we went to a house one couple had just moved into, he wanted me to make some scones, proper British baking and ever the people pleaser, I bought all the ingredients and busied myself in the kitchen while I heard him laughing and joking and smoking with his mates. The scones came out of the oven rock hard and tasteless. My skills weren't enough to win him over, and my shame and embarrassment were complete. He smiled consolingly at me as if it didn't matter, but it felt disingenuous and insincere. The others pretended to like them, but it was obvious they thought it was hilarious, and along with everyone else, he laughed. At me. At the *'English food'*, at the foreign girl who thought she could just walk back in when they knew he no longer cared, that he had moved on with one of them. I tried not to let it bother me. I pretended it was funny, it wasn't funny at all, it really hurt.

I don't remember much of that weekend. He was there, but he wasn't the soulmate I had left behind. He didn't end it between us. Instead, he kept me hanging on with vague promises to love me forever, to try and make it work. Skilfully swerving questions about visiting me in England, he showed zero interest in my course or university life, reluctant to sever all ties but unwilling to make any effort.

The brain and the heart are connected and disassociated at the same time. My heart cracked at the loss, and my brain reasoned with me to let go. Convincing myself that this was all my doing for selfishly returning to England, I had to put up and shut up, carrying around an enormous sense of guilt at the 'perfect' love I had binned so callously. I had little interest in meeting anyone or forming any sort of new relationship. I always let him know where I was living, writing with a new house number and ensuring he knew how to contact me.

On the off-chance…

He did call me, once, out of the blue. It had been almost two years, and when I heard his familiar voice, my heart dropped through to my legs. His tone was casual. He said he needed some information on a location in Covent Garden, for work. I was immediately and incredulously over the moon. Could we meet? When are you over? What sort of job? This was what I had dreamed and hoped for. He trailed off, mumbling about not being sure 'when', not sure 'if'. His voice faded out, and the words were vague soundbites – *if I could let him have the information that would be helpful, he needed that information, it was important* – the call ended awkwardly and with no plans other than for me to sort his request.

I had to finally face facts: he hadn't called for me at all. He had definitely moved on. My stupid heart made me put telegrams he had sent me, messages he'd written, silly drawings he'd made for me, and photos of our time together into an envelope—not to be opened, not to be looked at. It was too painful. I felt like a lovesick teenager and nothing like the mature economics student I was supposed to be. I closed the envelope, labelling and sealing it.

It was over.

At least for the next 18 years.

Chapter 6

Tout de Suite

That's not quite true. There was just one more time when we met. Very briefly.

I was living in the (famously) most romantic city in the world, studying for part of my degree. I had chosen to live in Paris for three months of my course. If I am totally honest, I wanted to recreate a part of how I felt when I lived in Rome, but it didn't quite work out because as feminine and pretty as Paris was - with the delicate sounding names and the most beautiful pastry shops, curly intricate street lamps and Métro signs straight out of a film noir - it didn't leave me breathless the way Rome had done. The Italian capital with its powerful and majestic buildings, noisy, musical and in-your-face people and colourful *Pizza al Taglio* hole-in-the-wall backstreet locations selling slices of savoury, doughy goodness. I'd lost my heart to that place. I appreciated the beauty of Paris; I just didn't love it.

So there I was, with a part-time job, a great social life and mediocre attendance at the university classes. I still wasn't over him, but that didn't stop casual flings mixed with plenty of alcohol: needs must and all that. I just held off from any deep and meaningful relationship. I lived in an apartment in Buzenval, a few Métro stops from the centre —nothing glamorous, but it was good enough. I shared a flat with a fellow university student who was a shining example of how to study and integrate yourself into Paris student life. Most of my time was spent hanging out with the staff at the pub I worked in near Rue St. Germain.

One evening, out of the blue, when I was at home, the telephone rang. Him. I almost dropped the phone when I heard his voice. '*I am here,*' he said. '*Here in Paris.*' Tentatively, he asked if I could meet him at his hotel. It would be much easier if I could go there for a few hours. He sounded excited at the possibility, and without a moment's hesitation, I changed clothes and prepared to go out, barely able to breathe, let alone explain to my flatmate what I was doing. I collected a few things, flew out of the apartment, and then grabbed a taxi to the other side of Paris – not cheap, but what price true love?

I arrived at a very imposing state-of-the-art hotel, and there he was, waiting for me at the entrance. The feeling was overwhelming. He had called me. He was in Paris for one night and had immediately thought of me and wanted to see me. I could hardly believe it. My heart was bursting with joy.

We said a quick hello to his various friends dotted around the hotel. They seemed slightly awkward to see me, but I didn't care, I was walking on a cloud. A drink or something to eat would have been lovely, but we didn't have much time, and he hurried me up to his hotel room so we could make the most of the couple of hours we had together. I naively thought we could spend the night there, but he said he had a very early flight, so I needed to leave. I called another taxi I could barely afford. Feeling disappointed, I hid it well. I mean, what can you do? It wasn't his fault that he needed to fly out on holiday.

On my way out, I stood on a map of the world etched on the floor of the hotel foyer; I looked at him and said, '*Wherever I am in the world, I will be thinking of you.*'

He nodded and smiled, empty of all expression. He had already turned to go.

Chapter 7

The One?

The obsession over meeting The One is definitely a thing, right? Or did it used to be a thing?

Modern supermarkets all have broader and longer aisles and more choices to accommodate the endless varieties of the same product with similar or identical ingredients. The only difference is the unique packaging, identifying that particular product as special enough for a starring role on the front of the shelf. Does modern dating work the same way? Those with exceptionally long, shiny hair go to the top of the most requested list. Cute dimples? Perfect teeth? Sparkly eyes? Maybe, just maybe, there is a little bit too much choice now when it comes to that ultimate quest of finding someone to love. It does seem to centre more around first impressions rather than your salt content.

Who cares if they are *The One* as long as they look polished, have excellent LinkedIn and Insta (definitely not Insta***gram***) profiles and know the best places to drink alcohol-free cocktails accompanied by vegan crisps. Is there less pressure or more now? Less, I suppose, because they are all replaceable. A conveyor belt of possibles, potentials or inbetweeners while you test them out, hoping you will eventually come across the right person for you. It isn't just appearance that's being critically appraised. With a gladiatorial style rating, the swipes come with other strict criteria—never mind being able to *tick* the right boxes, the potential other half could be carelessly admitting to any number of *'icks'*—from a love of crystals and horoscopes to how you take your coffee or park your car—unknowingly activating an instant dismissal and block.

A veritable minefield and a whole world away from meeting at the bus stop or exchanging landline numbers on bits of paper with times to call when your parents might be out. In the olden days, we would spend school days calculating percentages of true love based on the number of corresponding letters using our names. As we grew up, the question was, have we met them already? Was the one who got away actually The One? (confusing, I know) What if you met someone, and it all felt great, but a sliver of doubt crept in? You were too young, he lived on the wrong side of town, so you go with someone else and then spend years wondering what if.

Life wasn't so much complicated as fraught with the fear of making the wrong decision, and there was no digital footprint then, luckily or unluckily (*decidedly* lucky, I reckon). You made a decision then and there: no Facebook stalking, no checking their social media posts to track them or keeping your fingers crossed that you would bump into them at the next gaming convention. The most you could expect when I was growing up was something in the post, a handwritten missive requesting, remonstrating or pleading to get back together: that or a French kiss on the dance floor during the last slow record at the disco. As you smugly circled with his arms wrapped tight around you, those not quite as 'fortunate' watched on from the perimeter, excluded from the gang of desirables sucking each other's faces on the dancefloor.

Different times.

My taste in the opposite sex could be described as questionable. It wasn't always terrible, but when I did meet someone decent, I invariably messed it up. Nice guy who adored me? It would be great for a while, then, not so much. That could be down to maternal influences constantly reminding me that, as a result of being heavily invested in private education, I could definitely 'do better'. Or it could have been me, displaying a preference for someone the parents would disapprove of and then being surprised when that imploded.

It's crunch time, this whole concept of meeting The One. *If you know, you know* allegedly. Really? Know what exactly? That this is the person you want to spend the rest of your life with, have kids with, buy a house with? How can you know that in your teens, twenties, or even thirties? If you do know, that is astonishing, and congrats if it worked out; I must have incredibly poor judgement.

When I met 'him', I finally understood what everyone had been talking about, but true to form, I messed it up by leaving. I only had myself to blame.

Chapter 8

Frogs

I left university with a degree in European Economics and French, a wobbly heart and a sizeable debt.

Money: comforting, worrying, enjoyable, frightening. It covers all bases and, indeed, is the basis for most of what we do, and yet we disassociate ourselves from it as much as possible, claiming disinterest, embarrassment or secrecy. Like so many people, I have linked it directly to worry and stress, the rising fear marching hand in hand with the realisation that there isn't enough coming in to match the outgoings. And yet, long before I ever embraced the concept of the universe providing for me, I always figured I would find a way. Not via a lottery win, but I would find the solution to pay for what I wanted, needed or desired. I wasn't so much reckless as determined; even at university, I'd put aside the stress of an increasing overdraft if that Ghost dress was calling my name and worry about how to pay for it with a part-time job afterwards. Which I always managed to do.

Leaving university with an overwhelming student loan to pay off was only partially a result of my retail habit. During non-lecture days and holidays, I secured a job in a high-end clothes shop, using the money earned to maintain my love of fashion. I eventually paid off the student debt many years after I had finished my course, taking a large chunk of my monthly salary. Still busy trying to figure out what to do, I threw myself into each job; bar work, bar management and administration roles, all to build up my CV and keep those monthly payments chipping away at my overdraft.

At this time, I was on a mission to see if I could forget my relationship blunder by endlessly snogging (and sleeping with) completely unsuitable men and boys. After all, the breakup had been my decision, my need to better myself had ultimately ended us, I convinced myself that my selfish behaviour had finished the dream. Instead of rationalising my choice, I pushed that big, chunky piece of guilt to the back of my mind and carried on punishing myself by believing that no one was going to be right for me, because let's face it, I had let the perfect one go and I took full responsibility for that; as punishment, all I deserved was to 'kiss' the frogs.

Then I married one, but his prospects of turning into a handsome prince were low. He was a nice enough Essex boy, as far removed from my Italian dream as possible. Well, looks aren't everything, are they? Talk about damning with faint praise.

He wasn't exactly my type, but what is a type? Traits you have been conditioned to love or told are suitable for you, according to what and whom I have no idea.

Out of the mouth of (at the time) Prince Charles, I was pretty sure I loved him, *'whatever love means'*, indeed. Hands up, if I had been questioned under duress, I may have buckled and admitted that while I thought he was great, he wasn't the dream I'd had all my life. But dreams can be terribly unrealistic, and on paper, it all *seemed OK* —I was of marrying age and desperately wanted a baby, as did he, and we seemed compatible. Uh-oh! *'Seemed'* is not a great word when it comes to a lifelong commitment. We don't accept a marriage proposal saying *Well, yes, that seems like a good idea* however I wanted this relationship, and I was definitely in it long-term because, as far as I was concerned, marriage is for life, unlike a relationship where you can just jump on a plane and leave. A legal document tying you together, so you had to make it work.

He was a normal guy, an ambitious, steady in-a-decent-job type of bloke, offering the suburbia-ever-after I had blithely ignored until now. My parents breathed a sigh of relief that their wayward daughter had finally settled. Not entirely a blanket approval; after all, he came from Essex. Still, in that grand life plan where wedding, babies and a lifetime of domesticity followed, they were assured that I would at least be in the same country. As a runner-up prize, he was accepted. Just.

Married life wasn't an easy ride out of the financial wilderness either, nor had I expected it to be. My debt, my problem— fair enough, as he earned far more than I did, keeping it safe, apparently saving for 'our' future. He took charge, so our spending was frugal, and savings made where possible. On one memorable occasion, we plaster boarded a ceiling in the house together, a thankless, back-breaking task to save money despite his hatred of DIY and his 100k salary.

When trying unsuccessfully for a baby, I left a higher-salaried job in London as an office manager to take on a 'less stressful' (not necessarily so) job in a children's nursery closer to home. When Ol' Bandy Legs saw my first pay slip, he fell about laughing as I was earning less than he paid in tax. I felt embarrassed, but having pots of money didn't motivate me; security did, and I thought, until my divorce, that marriage would provide that. As it turned out, we weren't exactly on the same page on what marriage means.

Cancelling our IVF rounds and running off with someone else ended up being quite the deal breaker. When we went to court over financial issues, having put by all of 'our' money for months, he managed to simultaneously plead poverty while being represented by the most expensive legal team money could buy. I knew it was game over when his very expensive barrister stood up and declared that I was not entitled to anything as, and I quote, 'The wife had been unable to provide him with a child.' True enough, I had managed to miscarry twins, and subsequently, never conceived again. Rather than stick it out with me, he found someone fertile, and I added it to the other chunky piece of guilt stuffed into my subconscious. Having been almost ripped to shreds financially by someone who professed to *still have feelings for me* – yeah, me too – I managed to hold on to the house by the skin of my teeth; I bought him out and leased a room to a lovely lodger and started to re-think my life.

Things needed to change. I was back in a facilities management position but found it soul-destroying. The money was great, but something was missing. I wanted to travel, learn another language, and find somewhere where everything didn't revolve around money, where basics like education and food on the table were the priorities, not how big your house was and how many rooms and which fancy brand name you had on the back of your jeans. I took a part-time course in teaching English as a foreign language and started looking up potential volunteering positions as far away as possible. I was not running away.

Yeah right.

I was running away as fast as I could from all my bad decisions, the relationships I was evidently no good at. I was running hard to get away from those who surrounded me and had a 'normal life' (the kind of life I was desperate for) with small, beautiful kids running around, a big kitchen and a supportive partner. Disney scenarios. Crikey, I was even envious of the filing systems these friends of mine had with dental appointment cards and school dates all logged and kept in an orderly fashion. Everything I had longed for. I didn't want that shoved in my inadequate face anymore.

Chapter 9

Coffee? Tea? Me?

Was I feeling sorry for myself? Very much so, but I wouldn't and couldn't admit it.

Pretending instead I was OK with going away, but the truth was I felt totally lost. I didn't belong anywhere; friends had their mother and baby groups, were travelling or happily coupled up planning weddings. All I had ever wanted was a baby, and I had managed to fail spectacularly at that. It was 2006, and according to my medical file, I was a 'geriatric mother'. Time was slipping past, so I decided to take matters into my own hands.

I had a shed load of love to give, geriatric or not.

It was hard going back home and sitting in the front room telling my parents. My dad had tears in his eyes as I explained my need to go somewhere and do something different in a place I had never been. He was an old-school gentleman, still reeling from the cowardly behaviour of someone he had believed had his daughter's best interests at heart. He was from the generation which believed in marriage as something you fight for, something to be worked at. I gave them the geographical options—two places I had been offered year-long contracts—an orphanage on the Thai/Burmese border or teaching guides and groups of children in a cloud forest in Central America. My dad listened intently, and I could tell he had concerns about potential dangers in Burma (now Myanmar). Above all, I didn't want to worry him, Nicaragua it was then. Terrified and excited, I threw myself into this adventure like I did everything. As my mother was fond of saying, '*She could sell ice cream to the Eskimos, that one.*' This was not necessarily a compliment, but hinted at my single-mindedness—I couldn't be swayed once my mind was made up. She wasn't wrong.

Flights, airports and organisation I could do, but I was scared shitless of arriving in a totally unknown place and having to find my way to the northern town from where I had been given complicated instructions to take a chicken bus. This was giving me sleepless nights. Fortunately for me, another volunteer teacher came to the rescue. Responding to my pleas for help, he assured me he would come down from the north to meet me in Nicaragua's boiling hot, noisy, dirty capital of Managua. I felt relief and a creeping confidence that I could actually do this.

On my last night at home, my two best friends sifted through my rucksack, removing any clothes they deemed unnecessary. Holding up a chocolate brown linen shift dress, one of them raised her eyebrows, looking at me. '*Why in god's name do you think this is going to be essential in the middle of a cloud forest?*' Without missing a beat, I replied, '*Church, of course.*' In hysterics, they removed it and put it in the large bag which would arrive a few months after me. I was going to miss my people so much.

Landing in Nicaragua, I felt a rising sense of adventure and excitement. The volunteer who came to meet me made me feel immediately at ease. He was relaxed and familiar with everything, including the language, and patiently answered all my questions. Ultimately, he became a very good friend, and our Friday catch-up sessions were to provide a lifeline for me.

Once in Esteli (the last main town before heading up into the mountains), we queued to catch the chicken bus I was to become very familiar with. That very first time, it was like nothing I had ever seen before—a yellow US school bus packed to the rafters with people who took staring to a whole new level (Italians take note). People squeezed sacks of rice, coffee, beans, live chickens and cans of petrol into every square inch available. Passenger comfort was secondary, if not tertiary, with the primary goal to transport as much as possible to their families in the outlying communities. The people on board were all shapes and sizes, and personal space hadn't yet been invented. The bus swung speedily and precariously through the streets, horn blaring as it alerted any late arrivals of its departure. Eventually, it turned off to cross the river and slowly climbed toward the cloud forest.

Every so often, the bus stopped arbitrarily, dropping off passengers and whatever belongings they had crammed in. The radi was consistently thumpingly loud, spewing out tinny 80s ballads. Pushed up against a back window, with various Nicaraguans trying to find out who I was and where I was from in a language I felt I didn't have a hope in hell of ever understanding, let alone speaking. I looked out of the window at a view which resembled the film set of Jurassic Park—a vibrant changing landscape. The higher we climbed the more the terrain became rich with vegetation I had never seen before, massive trees and more shades of greens than a Pantone shade card. Bonnie Tyler rasped hoarsely through the bus speakers, still, apparently 'Lost In France'.

If only I was, I thought.

I arrived at the top of the cloud forest amid a stunning landscape. The bus was far lighter now. No longer weighed down with groceries and passengers, it picked up speed, happily cannoning around the dirt road bends at breakneck speed. I could feel the butterflies rising as I tightly gripped the top of the seat in front. Alone on the bus except for the driver, I prayed the family would be there to meet me.

I needn't have worried.

Climbing down the bus steps in the dusk, I could see three teenage girls and a man (their father presumably) running towards me, shouting and waving. Grabbing my bags between them, we set off towards the breeze block house. Mumbled introductions were made inside, as only those who don't speak each other's language can do, and then they took me into my room. My hand immediately went to the left to look for the light switch—rookie mistake. No electricity. The youngest came in behind me, cradling a candle on a plate, and then they left me to it. I sat on the edge of the mosquito net-covered bed, looked at the grey walls and took in the wooden windows.

In that moment, I felt a small knot of panic rise in my throat and tears threatened. I gave myself a stern bollocking, *'Don't you dare bloody cry, this is what you wanted, you chose to do this, no one forced you into this. Do* ONE WEEK, *and if you really hate it, then you can leave.'* It worked. I took a deep breath and joined the family at the table, where they had set me a place, and I ate the dinner they had prepared for me. Taking it one day at a time and heeding the advice given by established volunteers, I organised English classes, learnt how to ride a horse to teach in different communities, and attended social gatherings despite not understanding a single word. It would happen, the language thing, I was confident of that.

My first few months were tough, but it wasn't all bad. Heading back to the main town every Friday on the bus was a great break from the remote cloud forest. Flushing toilets, intermittent internet access and weekly fresh fruit and pancakes with my American friend, regaling each other with absurd tales of community life. Bizarrely, it was all starting to feel almost normal, and I was no longer afraid of the consequences of giving up because I had no intention of doing so. I didn't know where it was all leading, but that was also ok with me. I was sure I would find out soon enough. Anything I had planned so far had repeatedly slapped me in the face, so I was willing to leave things to chance.

Basics and money, as it turned out, have the same value wherever you are.

Community and neighborly rivalries abounded: the depth of the well for your toilet hole, the state of the flower-edged path leading directly through your garden towards the outdoor shower made of concrete with a bowl and a bucket of cold water. The kitchen fire standards they all aspired to (essential for all cooking needs, from homemade tortillas to roasting the coffee beans): Did you have the one spewing smoke back into your kitchen? Or did the smoke expel properly up through the chimney and out through the hole in the roof? It all mattered.

Vegetables, flowers, and medicinal herbs grown on family plots inspired jealous rivalry, territorial attitudes and fierce levels of competition not restricted solely to their gardens. Appearances were noted and judged, such as who had the sleekest, smoothest hair, the whitest trainers, the loveliest makeup. The bus ride into town every Friday morning for the weekend was an exercise in showing off new jeans, painted nails and suffocating perfume: a veritable catwalk show. Travel may broaden the mind, but people are fundamentally the same, give or take.

Aside from general chit-chat, the main subject invariably revolved around their most valued and precious product: coffee. Up and down the hills and mountains and across the cloud forest, the arabica plants which grew everywhere looked relatively unassuming to an untrained eye. But to the coffee producers, these were the lifeblood of their communities and a key source of income for most families. Despite no clear boundary lines between the plants, everyone seemed to know down to the last twig who owned what. Never mind *Where's Wally?* Their knowledge and accuracy were remarkable. I had picked coffee a couple of times and found it to be an exhausting, thankless task, but one where entire communities worked alongside each other to harvest the ripe red coffee cherries. With radios slung from their necks and homemade straw baskets, they cheerfully spent hours picking, laughing and gossiping until their sacks were brimming, weighed and then transported back to be emptied and the beans laid out to dry.

The women's cooperative was by far and away the liveliest; their meetings a viper's nest of gossip and accusations. I spent my time between various groups, learning the language, getting to know people and trying to understand what was needed. Most believed in further education. They understood it was a means for a better future.

The idea, as most good ones do, happened purely by accident—backpackers, I salute you. Four months after arriving, my best friend visited me. Making the most of her time with me, I showed her as much as we could fit in, including heading west to the university city of León, home to students, backpackers and hostels, international cuisine, a stunning Pacific coastline, and volcanoes. It was a world away from the staid northern town I had been used to, just five bus hours up the road. Friendly groups from around the world searched for the real deal, an authentic Central American experience, and here I was, with the key. When backpackers exchange stories, it is usually about where they are headed next. I was quite the oddball. I *lived* there. Automatically, people were intrigued. They wanted in. They wanted to make tortillas, fetch water from the well, sit on that chicken bus and do yoga in the moonlight.

This was the start, having convinced my friends in the community that, yes, there were people who wanted the full 'Nica' experience: sleeping and eating with a local family, helping out with day-to-day tasks. We fixed prices, the families prepared rooms, and I regularly travelled down to León to seek out potential customers and bring them back up. It worked, it really worked. The families had an extra source of income, which they invested in improving their homes and expanding their coffee-growing, while the backpackers lapped up cloud forest life.

I was delighted, and one good idea led to another...

All the houseguests commented on how delicious the coffee was, and sensing another income opportunity, we packaged the freshly roasted coffee for them to take home. Every weekend, I packed a load into a rucksack and every weekend headed to León on the bus to promote and sell the packs to bars, hostels and restaurants. Oh, remember that brown linen shift dress I had to wait for? One night in León, I was out having a drink with a surf-obsessed backpacker, wearing the dress, and I explained what I did out there. Looking at me, he said, 'So, you must be the *coffee fairy*.'

The maths was simple: Amazing Coffee + International Sales = Better Deals for Farmers and Improved Educational Facilities.

All I had to do was cut out the middle man, export the coffee directly and help improve and increase educational facilities in the cloud forest. The Coffee Fairy was born. Off I went, in a fog of often pretend happiness, worry, and people-pleasing. I didn't have a clue what I was doing, just with blind faith that it was right. Fundamentally, I had found something for me, and I could feel myself gaining in confidence as I confronted each problem and seemingly insurmountable obstacle and found a way. There were times when I wished I could share it with someone, but knowing what to do or coming up with a solution was also part of going it alone, and I embraced that.

* * *

I was never interested in dating anyone from the Nicaraguan community. They were mostly all married off in their late teens, and after my year was up, I was still going back twice a year to sort the coffee, build and paint school rooms and buy resources. Becoming involved with someone would be complicated and could compromise my position in the community, I had built up their trust, and I wanted and needed to maintain it.

When at home in England , I tried internet dating; everyone seemed to be using it, but following a run of major fails, I was about to give up when, predictably, I did meet someone: ex-military, a tall, softly spoken, gorgeous blue-eyed Welshman, shy, kind and gentle—a man who had the nerve to treat me as if I was someone special. Clever, articulate, polite and funny, he did everything he possibly could to make me happy. I was having none of it. An internal battle ensued. I wasn't used to this and was pretty sure I didn't deserve it. I fought hard against my heart and my body, both all in and rejoicing that I had finally met someone wonderful. Unfortunately, my head had other ideas, told me I knew best. I rejected him continuously, constantly batting away his efforts to show how much he loved me, finding fault and picking arguments to prove that I certainly didn't love him (I certainly did). Eventually, exhausted by me and my ridiculous ways, he left me to it. I couldn't blame him. Was he the one who got away? Maybe, or maybe he just had a lucky escape. I will never know.

At the start of 2011, I decided to give online dating a wide berth. Everyone of an age I considered suitable (late 30's to late 40's) were optimistically throwing themselves in the direction of fertile twenty-something-year-old-fresh-faced-poppets. The last person I had risked a lunch date with had shown up in minus temperatures, sockless with open shoes. I wasn't so pretentious I would judge someone on their footwear alone, but when he called me a couple of days later and told me that he *'knew me better than I knew myself'*, I gently put the phone down on him and decided the single life was decidedly less complicated.

So there I was, over in some remote coffee plantation, negotiating transport deals, measuring sacks of beans, buying paint for schools I had built and interviewing farmers for the BBC *Food Programme*. I was with a wonderful photographer friend and things were going really well.

Life, for me, was about to turn on its axis.

Chapter 10

You can run but you can't hide

My entire focus was the business, a great distraction that kept me busy and made me feel needed – challenging, satisfying although not terribly lucrative, but that had never really been my motivation. I was more than OK, even happy, and I couldn't really ask for anything else. Trips to Nicaragua to talk to the farmers and sort the educational resources and funding, building schools and toilets and providing water filters, I loved it even if at times it was lonely and hard work. When I was back in the UK, I travelled around giving talks in schools about coffee-growing communities and attending coffee fairs, climbing that learning curve of where to place my coffee beans in an already saturated market.

Enlisting the help of countless amazing friends from all over the world helped keep me sane. The competition to make, sell, and promote coffee was tough, but in various fairs and exhibitions my friends could explain the origins and keep their wits about them as I came frequently close to losing mine while putting up with endless 'coffee experts' hiding amongst the general public. It was fulfilling, exhausting and, at times, the best fun I have ever had.

* * *

I was in that northern Nicaraguan town in early 2011 when I opened the email.

The six million dollar question I didn't even realise I had been holding my breath waiting for: *'Are you the girl who used to go out with...?'* Yep, in the Nicaraguan mountains, through the power of the internet, my past had finally caught up with me. His friend sent the message because *he* didn't know how to use the internet. Apparently, during a conversation about past relationships, I had been the one he had always wondered about. Where was I, and what had become of me? Not having a clue how to track me down, his mate had come to his rescue. I replied, not daring to believe it was true. I left my email details, and before long, he replied.

I had never allowed myself to hope, never dared to. That thing about your legs buckling? That happened. They felt like they couldn't support me, and I had to sit down. My legs might not have been working, but the smile on my face definitely was as I read the words in Italian.

Subject: How wonderful to have found you again!!

Hello, you fantastic person, finally I have found you, while I write this I am overcome with feelings.

The emotions running through my head reading that sentence were overwhelming. It was as if I had finally won first prize; it had taken time, but this is who I had been waiting for, and I had been right to wait. I needed someone who really knew me, someone who had been there when I was in my twenties, someone who could look at me now and know what I had been like, looked like. This was what everyone else had, that relationship with The One; now I, too, could have it. True love in every sense of the word, and I would give it my everything. I believed in it as much in that moment as I had nearly twenty years ago, because this time I was determined there would be no more mistakes.

I called him a few days before leaving to fly back home. Hearing his deliciously familiar voice for the first time in nearly two decades hit every spot within me, and we talked about everything and nothing. It didn't seem real, yet it was real and happening. He was living by the beach just south of Rome. Things had been tricky work-wise as the worldwide recession hit, but he was OK. It was just a question of time before he found work again. *'I would give anything to see you,'* he told me, but he didn't know how that would work so I made it happen. On ending the call, I booked a flight to Italy. Telling him I would be over within two weeks, I basked in his admiration: *'Finally,'* he said, *'someone who does what they say they are going to do.'* I felt as if I had been awarded a shiny gold star.

This was the ending I had wished, hoped and dreamed of but never believed could happen. Back home, we tried to talk as much as possible, as he had found a way to access Skype, explaining how much he had spent to make it possible to connect virtually with me. I was blown away by how much he was putting himself out to spend money and learning about technology just to be in constant contact with me. He didn't have to do any of it.

Everything pointed to us having found the missing piece of our puzzle.

During our calls, the language I had struggled with initially came back to me as familiar as my mother tongue as I pushed it through the Spanish and practised words I had long since buried. Our conversations were about our life before and occasionally veered to the intimate and personal; once, when he asked if one of my breasts still pointed out to one side, I was shocked and felt more than a little humiliated. He started laughing, but sensing my discomfort and embarrassment, he stopped himself and reassured me it was one of the things he loved about me, and that was why he had remembered.

I felt silly for being so sensitive; he was just being adorable.

I couldn't wait to see him and watch the future we were destined to have finally unfold.

Chapter 11

Finders Keepers

As I parked up in Gatwick that cold March day in 2011 and switched off Mr Vine's programme, I set off to find the Happy Ever After of my own true love story. Only a few very close friends knew what I was planning to do and who I was going to see. Overjoyed at the thought of such a romantic escapade, we had talked incessantly about the potential physical delights waiting for me after all these years. There was no doubt in anyone's mind: *Italians Do It Better*. The anticipation was positively mouthwatering. They were very much looking forward to me reporting back.

The decision to keep it relatively quiet – despite wanting to shout it from the rooftops – was not because of any doubts or fears I may have had but more to do with my unconventional life and the way it had so far raised more than a few eyebrows. I hadn't exactly followed the traditional route of marriage, husband, babies and a steady, safe, salaried job – not for lack of trying. My fear was that such an unorthodox meet-up could be met with a cynicism or scepticism, and I was weary of not 'fitting in'. Instead, I wanted to hold on tightly to this nugget of precious information, hold it close to my heart until it had properly set into an indestructible hardened rock no one could break.

Not this time.

I walked through the packed terminal with crazy butterflies in my stomach, feeling a strange mix of confidence and shyness. I was overwhelmed at the crowds, having fantasised this meeting a million times with the image of me strolling through a deserted gate and seeing him standing there alone, waiting for me. Instead, it turned out that Rome had become a very much sought after destination in the last twenty odd years, and as the international gateway to this capital city, the airport was understandably rammed. I walked slowly through the crowds and panicked as I couldn't immediately pick him out, and then suddenly, I glimpsed a flash of yellow, and there he was. That was when the crowds seemed to disappear around us and he stood there holding a bunch of flowers with the biggest, goofiest and widest grin. Familiar and welcoming, he was almost exactly as I remembered him.

He had left his car parked haphazardly in a no-parking area at the airport and was keen to move it before he was caught. Grabbing me in a half hug, we ran giggling through the crowds, holding onto each other, almost falling over my case, both of us breathless, all adding to the very Italian madness of the moment. Driving back to his apartment by the sea, sneaking glances at each other in utter disbelief, finally back together again, those young people who had once owned Rome. I gripped onto his hand for the duration of the journey, and he never once let go. I read the road signs we passed, pronouncing the place names and rolling the letters around in my mouth —names I had put to the back of my mind for those two decades. Everything felt surreal, not so much fireworks as romantic pink bubbles pinging off in the air all around us.

At his place, I went into the bathroom, stared for a few minutes at my reflection, and decided I was dreaming, so I pinched myself. It couldn't be real, yet when I opened the door and leaned my head out to double-check, there he was, waiting for me looking equally disbelieving.

I unpacked and handed him the precious memories I had kept for so long. He was speechless when he saw the pack of photos, handwritten messages, drawings, and even the telegram he had sent. Wanting to demonstrate a similar romantic nostalgia, he showed me that he had kept a soft navy blue T-shirt I had bought him. It was falling to bits, but to me, it was authentic confirmation that he had never stopped loving me. An old Calvin Klein T-shirt, a present brought back from a holiday, lovingly kept, a reminder of a time once shared. Proof.

We spent the next few days feeling our way around, literally and figuratively. After so long apart, I couldn't wait to catch up on our lives and share, explain, talk and listen. I wanted to know everything. On the other hand, he was reticent and far less keen to share his story. I figured he was shy, plus there was still a slight language barrier, and it had been such a long time. I also suspected he was embarrassed because he didn't have a job and was more than likely feeling humiliated about his financial situation. My heart went out to him, and I was keen to put him at his ease, allowing him to take his time and open up to me, gradually and gently coaxing him to tell me what he had been doing with his life while I told him about me.

After all these years of wondering, I was fascinated to hear his story.

He had followed his dream into fashion and worked alongside *that* girlfriend for almost ten years as a visual merchandiser in a relatively famous retail chain, apparently very successfully. After working in Italy and around Europe, he wanted to be his own boss, so he ended up owning an independent clothing store in this beach town. Eventually, he was accepted by the locals and enjoyed moderate success. Unfortunately, he had been seeing someone at the time who told him she would take care of his accounts, and he had trusted her to do so. Frowning as he remembered the chaos she managed to create, I listened, appalled. The details activated my sense of injustice and an overwhelming feeling of protection towards him. What exactly had she done? How had she done it? I was outraged. He looked bewildered, struggling to remember the details and shaking his head. He said it made him too angry to go over it all, to relive it. The bottom line was he had to let his business go to pay for the mess she had made. In a climate of economic national unease, with the new euro and acts of terrorism triggering a worldwide recession resulting in severe unemployment, life had not been easy for him.

I sympathised as I had always been told I was terrible with numbers, and true enough, maths has been my nemesis throughout life. However, this poor man had his livelihood destroyed by someone he had put his faith in, which was beyond cruel.

In other intimate and heartfelt conversations, I brought up the subject of our initial relationship and how much time we had lost by not remaining together. He was adamant it would have failed and that it was not the right time for us. I disagreed because I believed it would have worked, but I said nothing because I didn't want to shatter the perfect moment. He was still friends with *that* ex-girlfriend, my 'replacement' back then. I didn't like it, but I kept quiet. Nor did we discuss the betrayals or infidelities as it was a long time ago; we were different people then, so I followed his lead and avoided it, too, not wanting to re-open old wounds.

He told me he had been in contact with her since we had been back together and had called her because he wanted to share the news about us. My mouth fell open as he told me she had guessed he was seeing someone from the happiness in his voice. Laughing at my expression, he said that he had told her his joy resulted from him being back with the true love of his life.

That is how he told her.

Now, I wasn't on phone call terms with any of my exes, but try as I might, I couldn't picture myself telling someone I had spent many years with that, despite our time together, I was truly happy to be back with my *true* love. I put it down to him having had a much easier personality and the fact he was far more laid back, so, in general, his relationships had smoother endings. He reassured me that they were, in fact, just good platonic friends, and she was now settled down and happily married with two gorgeous children. This served only to increase my curiosity: why hadn't he wanted to marry her and have children? He shrugged noncommittally, *'It wasn't to be. Just one of those things.'* Despite my outwardly blasé reaction to this news, I continued asking polite questions about her life and her children, while inside, I was dancing the jiggiest jig of joy at this news. I felt a warm childish delight wrap me up in a sweet candy-floss pillow of comfort and love; yes, I am well aware that sounds like a pile of saccharine guff, but the fact was he had called her and told her I was the *'love of his life'*, that it had *always* been me, little old me! After years apart, including a decade spent with her, it turned out that he had never forgotten the greatest love of his life (notwithstanding the yawning distance between us), and he had confirmed it in a call to her.

I apologise for my lack of female solidarity but I wasn't going to waste any time on compassion. She had shown little compunction when it came to moving in on him in the first place, so it wasn't for me to feel sorry for the woman. That all-encompassing feeling of joy stayed with me like a Ready Brek outline for the entire duration of my stay. I was buzzing. These few days were more than I could have ever hoped for—verification, validation endorsement and recognition. All the big words, and all for me, the person who had been treated so shabbily, I was suddenly on the most wanted list, in a good way—in a very, very good way.

Not working out quite as effortlessly, however, was the intimate side of things.

Surprisingly and somewhat disappointingly, I realised that contrary to those fashionable logos, Italians don't actually do it better. Turns out they could benefit from a decent manual explaining the give as well as the take side of things. I mean, it was *pretty good* – you could even describe it as frequent and frenetic, but amazing? Naaah.

Disappointingly, the kissing was well below average, a really disheartening factor for me because I'm a big fan of smooching properly, a demonstratively loving part of affection. So much can be expressed through a kiss: intimacy, love and playfulness, all vital statistics in the sexy stuff. It should never be underestimated and can change from a peck to full-on necking in a matter of seconds, which is why I am such a fan.

His kissing wasn't the best, but he admitted that and seemed happy for me to show him. He wanted to learn, but it was a work in progress; anything I taught him was quickly forgotten. He made the right moves and very obviously desired me, but he was impatient for the extras to be over as they took a bit too much effort and could easily be dispensed with. Why waste precious minutes on appetisers and side dishes when the main course was available?

I had no issue with practice making perfect because a relationship built on good sex was only part of it, and we were going to have so much fun exploring likes and dislikes and getting to know each other, it could be something we'd work on together, and how much fun would that be?! I mean, look what I had, for god's sake! The love of my life, my tall, gorgeous, kind and loving soulmate, so I could hardly be worried about a bit of kissing not measuring up.

I needed to chill out, be less *exacting*, and learn the meaning of patience and compromise because it was clear from those first few heady days that we had time and were not some *flash in the pan*. I was confident and secure in the knowledge that, gradually, we would become so in tune that we would know exactly how to please each other and have the best time doing it.

At the end of those incredible few days, we went out for our last dinner. Holding hands over the table in this terribly romantic restaurant overlooking the sea, I shared stories of my hopes and dreams for the coffee company. I talked of how hard it had been, how I had hit rock bottom financially, and how I had been looking at cleaning jobs to try and supplement my income. Instead, I had found an investor and could see a way forward after my hard work and, hopefully, the commercial success I had dreamed of. He understood more than I could have imagined. Embarrassed and stammering a little, he shared *his* story of financial desperation.

Listening to him finally open up, I saw a vulnerable side that matched my own feelings and experiences. He, too, had needed to accept the worst sort of job following the closure of the shop. Struggling with a virtually non-existent employment market, he had even tried his hand as a night security guard at a local shopping mall. It had been dreadful, and I winced as I imagined him patrolling that place alone in the dark. Nightmarish, no wonder he had left. As he talked, I was struck by how much our lives had almost paralleled in terms of trying so hard. It had always been an uphill struggle, and we were alone trying to forge the career path we craved. Listening to him, I realised that in many respects, he had gone through a much worse time than me; I had by comparison, been very lucky. When he barely had the money for food, and all attempts to find work with everyone he knew had proved futile, he had been given contact details from *someone who needed someone*, and off he went, optimistic that this could be his big break. Ending up in a warehouse with a few other 'candidates' and several tough-looking individuals lined up to 'interview' them, he realised that, once again, this was not a suitable career choice, no matter how desperate he had become. He described how he and several others sat there listening to a group of Eastern Europeans hand out instructions regarding the delivery of packages. I listened in wide-eyed horror as, in a low voice, barely looking at me, he told me he decided it wasn't worth getting into, gave his excuses, and walked out.

I couldn't believe it. I was in awe of his bravery and conviction that, in terrifying circumstances, he had the strength and fortitude to trust his instincts. Most of all, I felt relief at not having lost him to the Albanian underworld. He had shown the same determination and courage as I had when faced with some of the bleakest situations. And in that puddle of a loved-up, people-pleasing brain, I squeezed his hand and told him, *'Together we are going to build our future, something where you will be happy and content in your chosen field of work. I will help you because you are a good man who deserves the best.'* I could see from his expression that he was just as relieved as I was that we met at exactly the right time.

We clung to each other in the car on the way to the airport. *'Maybe one day we could have a big party and invite lots of friends and family,'* I whispered to him. He looked at me tearfully and said, *'I've never wanted that with anyone until you.'*

Chapter 12

Soft Landing

That first year passed quickly in a haze of loved-up bliss while trying (and failing) not to be smug about it.

Reuniting with your soulmate after such a long time was astonishing in itself, but being so obviously suited to each other was mind-blowing—we appeared to have everything in common, from music to food to opinions, proving that even in this enlightened age, not only do we believe in fairytales, but we naturally fall for them too, over and over because ultimately it is what so many of us hope and wish for—a realistic fantasy.

He was beautifully talented at making me feel like his everything, his entire world. The fierce intensity was quite something, but he was Italian, and his nationality was renowned for it – passionate, demonstrative, over the top – a nation that took romance very seriously. Besides, I was more than OK with effusive and unrestrained after years without and happily absorbed it all. Cementing it was the history we shared, so it was hardly surprising that everything slipped into place so easily this time around. If I heard a particular song on the radio, I'd excitedly share that I had always thought of him whenever I had heard it. Looking at me in awe, with almost tears in his chocolate brown eyes and brimming over with love, he whispered, '*I can't believe it, I did too,*' and taking me in his arms, I fell a little further.

Was there any point at which I felt a tiny bit cynical? Did I doubt his sincerity at all? After all, I wasn't *that* naive was I? Of course, I love hearts and flowers like anyone, but I also appreciate a decent dose of reality. *'Really?'* I'd laugh at him. *'Did that really happen?'* or *'Do you honestly think that way?'* His reaction was so extreme it stopped me in my tracks. He would look downcast and sad and genuinely hurt. Immediately, I'd feel terrible for not believing *every* word he said, for being sceptical. *'Why do you think I would lie?'* he would ask me, astounded. *'I have no need to lie to you.'* I would feel ashamed and stupid I had doubted the one person in the entire world who felt nothing but absolute love for me. What kind of a person did that make me? Why could I not just accept this was real and wonderful and take it at face value? Hugging me tightly and accepting my grovelling apologies, he would comfort me, murmuring that I must have had some awful people in my life to be so suspicious. Chastened that he could forgive me so easily, I was determined to be less cynical, softer and more accepting.

No wonder everyone had left me.

An area where I definitely felt more comfortable was the bedroom. I was working hard at spin classes, looking more toned than I had been in years. I felt confident in my body and was keen to show it off. I felt relaxed around him and he certainly appreciated my efforts, regularly making a grab for parts of me, looking at me and asking, territorially, who they belonged to. *'Whose is this?'* he would gruffly say, half serious and half joking. I'd squirm in delight, thinking how much he loved me because it felt like the most romantic gesture ever. It meant he wanted me and wasn't afraid to show me how much. An almost desperate need to metaphorically possess me and I loved it. *I felt loved.* If I didn't answer correctly, he would grab me again and repeat the words 'Who. Does. This. Belong. To?' Demanding confirmation that I was all his.

He had found me all the way over on the other side of the world. We were both single, which made me feel even more secure because we couldn't hurt anyone. There was no one to leave for us to be together and no hearts broken in the timing of this perfect relationship. I was ripe to be loved unconditionally, and he was ready to be whatever I wanted and needed—my walking, talking, living dream boy. From family to friends to the lady who worked in the post office, they could all see how sparklingly happy he made me. It wasn't just the perfect ending for us, it was the happy ending everyone wanted for me. Concluding there was nothing left for him in Italy, he became committed to moving to the UK. With an entirely different attitude from the first time, he embraced all the changes, proving a newly found enthusiasm and maturity; now, he had goals, and everything pointed to us working together to find a way forward. It was a question of when, not if.

In the meantime, those wonderfully romantic trips between Italy and England genuinely deepened our love. It was exciting. The travelling back and forth seemed glamorous, and the difficult absences in between made us more determined. He loved it, too, because whenever we met, I brought a ton of presents for him, having spent my free time on the lookout for gifts which would make up for the fact that we were not always together—things I knew he would love or would make his life easier. Luckily, all these things were available in England and less expensive than in Italy. I had access to discounted designer labels at a shop called TK Maxx, which was fortunate, as his preference was for anything by Ralph Lauren. He had ruefully explained that cheap clothes didn't suit him, so I made it my goal to surprise him with amazing gifts at knockdown prices.

Showing me the one or two beautifully kept designer sweaters he'd owned for years, he demonstrated the care he took with his things. I nodded in agreement, squirrelling away in my memory his size in jumpers, jeans and trainers, like the female version of a year-round Father Christmas, happy that I would be spoiling him with exactly what he wanted. There is nothing quite like that demonstration of love when you hand over something and anticipate the delight and surprise—receiving presents is lovely, but the sheer joy of giving cannot be underestimated, a role I wholeheartedly embraced. He adored the shops in England, marvelling at the variety and availability, comparing them unfavourably to Italy, oohing and aahing at the price of his favourite multivitamins, moisturiser or preferred underpants.

He never actually asked me to buy anything, but said to keep an eye out and let him know if I came across the item. When I presented him with the gift, he was surprised and delighted while protesting: *'You shouldn't be spending your money on me.'* Insisting he'd be happy just walking along the beach or sharing a plate of pasta with me because he loved a simple life. *'Material things are nice enough, but they aren't everything,'* he would say. Yet more proof of what an incredibly humble and wonderful person he was, spurring me to do whatever it took to maintain his contentment and well-being.

When I visited his place at the beach in that small Italian town, he'd show me off to everyone – friends from way back, business owners, and people from the bars and restaurants. All of them welcomed me with open arms, and as far as I was concerned, it was further proof of what a lovely person he was, authentic, popular and loved. I basked in their warmth and generous hospitality, feeling very much at home with them all despite being regarded as something of a novelty; long lost love, the girl with a coffee business from the UK – out of nowhere, his life was turning around, and although they didn't doubt the sincerity of our love, because that was obvious for all to see, they were nonetheless slightly baffled. I couldn't figure out what was so difficult to comprehend. Once again, I found myself facing those 'raised eyebrows'. We had found each other, and we were sorting out the best way to make it work. What was the big deal? Why was it so difficult to accept our choices?

He knew the answer and had even been here before. It boiled down to their jealousy, he explained. They were envious of us. Now it was my turn to look baffled, so he broke it down for me, almost harshly; these people were stuck in a backwater town in a country economically on its knees with no ambition to move away to try something new. The irony was that they would love to leave, but ultimately, they lacked the courage. *'Envy is such a negative emotion,'* he would sigh, weary of such antipathy. *'People have always had a problem with how I seem to land on my feet.'* I nodded my head in agreement. I understood and was proud of his positivity and resilience in not allowing their somewhat judgmental attitude to bring him down. He was so bright, happy, and adventurous, willing to try anything to change his life to create a successful future. It was inevitable that such a positive mental attitude would encourage naysayers.

Everything pointed to a great future, and we both had the same perspective: nothing ventured, nothing gained. He frequently arranged for us to see old friends, lunches or dinners at their houses to socialise, chat and share memories, knowing how thrilled I was to see people who had been such a massive part of our previous lives. I felt more connected, like we'd come full circle. Now, they could see how we were always destined to be together. Our story had blipped, paused, and was now back on course, and we wanted to share it with everyone. He told me he felt sorry for many of them, stuck in their dead-end jobs without an exciting future—unlike us.

We met up in Milan on one occasion to visit friends who lived in the city and whom I hadn't seen for over twenty years. We were to meet at the airport and take the train into the centre together. On greeting him, I realised he had brought no money, nothing. He didn't see it as a problem because, apparently, we wouldn't need any. It just required me to cover the cost of the train tickets to the city centre and from there we could walk to his friends' apartment. Sorted. He was decidedly irritated at my flabbergasted reaction and dismissed any misgivings I had. I knew the score, knew he had no work and no money, so why would I make him feel even worse about something he was powerless to change?

This was a tricky moment. Why did I feel so bad? I had been invited to this weekend and had already covered the cost of both our flights. A meet-up with friends I had been so looking forward to now felt off. The idea that as a couple, we were staying in the home of his friends, eating, drinking and hanging out together but without making a single contribution was not normal to me. On countless occasions in the past, my ex-husband had made me feel inadequate about my earnings. I certainly didn't want to become that person and make him feel inferior, but something else was going on here – less to do with the lack of money because, although that carried a sting, I was really trying to be sympathetic and understanding, this was to do with my concerns being dismissed, my opinion deemed irrelevant.

The crack was tiny, but it was there, and I fell silent.

His reaction changed to apologetic and conciliatory. He was truly sorry about not having enough for the train tickets, but he did this *for me*, fixing everything because he thought I wanted to go to Milan. He shouldn't have been so thoughtless, and it wasn't fair of him to pressurise me, we could have seen them at any time, and he should have waited till he had more money. He felt embarrassed that he hadn't provided himself with some spending money, in fact he had tried. He didn't want to tell me, had wanted to surprise me; he had worked for a friend of his, but the friend had disappeared, unable to pay him, and he'd had to leave with nothing. He felt awful. So did I. He had done everything he could and had been let down. All I ever wanted was for him to try, and he had. I couldn't ask for more. They were his friends, and he knew what their expectations were. As he repeatedly told me, it had always been that way when he stayed with them, he never paid for anything. They were his best friends; they had loads of money and knew his situation. I deferred to him as he knew how these things worked. After all, they were his people, and it was his country.

I papered up that tiny crack with a big, huge smile of acceptance.

Chapter 13

The Grass is Always Greener

I don't believe I had ever felt more secure about my future.

The months leading up to his arrival in England were spent encouraging and bolstering his confidence, showing him job sites where openings he had only ever dreamed of in Italy were readily available. Promising help with applications and a CV in English, I shone with conviction and happiness; all he needed to do was learn enough of the language to start, and then it would all happen naturally. He, in turn, was generous with his calm reassurances, constantly telling me how things would be so much better for us both once we were living together. He wanted a job, any job, so he could start paying me back for everything I had already paid out, whatever it took, wherever. All he wanted was to provide for me and repay the faith I had shown. I couldn't wait to start a life with someone special, side by side, working together to achieve the life I longed for.

He was keen to move to a place where people were so much friendlier, where opportunity blossomed for those willing to grab it with both hands, this extraordinary place where the women didn't need to wear a full face of makeup or have regular Botox as they looked so fresh-faced and happy in their own skin. Regularly comparing it unfavourably with the appearance-obsessed, grumpy and insular Italians, there was very little he didn't love about England. On his visits, he walked around in wide-eyed wonder while I delighted in the compliments and his constant state of astonishment at the way things worked and how different, clean and polite he found it.

I introduced him to everyone I knew as I felt they couldn't help but be captivated by his natural charm, and I thought they could be a potential shoo-in for any small jobs to tide him over while his English improved. My constant, confident message to my circle was: *'Tell everyone he is coming here to live, looking for work and is willing to do anything'* leaving them wondering how they could help this enigmatic, good-looking Italian get back on his feet again.

I left in the mornings to go to work, and he familiarised himself with that small town in West Sussex, spending time in the numerous charity shops and coffee shops, becoming accustomed to life in rural England. When I returned home, he would regale me with the inabilities of the locals to make a decent espresso and then show off his new vocabulary and best attempt at English. *'Today, I saw a squitter,'* he said triumphantly, and then, seeing my confused face, he'd grab the picture dictionary he had found lying around and show me. *'See, a squitter.'* With tears of laughter running down my face, I would explain that the creature was, in fact, a squirrel, but he would be so delighted at my reaction that he refused to correct himself, saying it over and over again.

Television was no longer the relaxing couple of hours where you could switch off. Everything needed translating, but eventually, I found his perfect programme: *Grand Designs*. He adored that show, the renovations, the stunning results and the ability of people to *'think outside of the box'*, jokingly referring to his *'friend'* Kevin McCloud. I was, by proxy, ecstatic. Finally, we had found him something he liked watching, and it was a testament to his innate taste in style and design, with the added bonus he would learn English in no time by following the subtitles. I had picked up Spanish by doing the same in Nicaragua.

He tried but found it too fast, and those on screen tended to speak with strange accents, so you couldn't blame him for being unable to follow it. '*Not everyone finds languages easy*,' he gently admonished me, and I made another mental note to go easy on him. After all, he was embracing all things British as if it were a newborn baby, his baby, his discovery. I looked on proudly, seeing this transition working perfectly: my friends had already mentioned possible painting jobs. The language would come. In the meantime, I was full of optimism and hope.

His home country, on the other hand, had very much become the devil incarnate, the bad guy he didn't want to be around anymore. He frequently talked about the corruption and how dirty and crooked it was because nothing worked, from broken roads to unemployment. His vitriol towards Italy was understandable. Having tried everything, that place had totally let him down, no work, no financial assistance, no help whatsoever. Their loss was my gain. I was worried about him leaving his friends behind and his family, too, despite their irregular contact. Regardless of how happy he was to be moving, I wanted him to understand the reality because it was a huge undertaking. I needn't have worried, and he certainly didn't pull any punches when it came to explaining his mindset. His 'real friends' were very few, and the ones he had minimal contact with had their own lives and families, rarely visiting him. They certainly hadn't been there when things had been tough, good-time friends who only showed up when things were going well. I found this difficult to hear because my own friends had always been loyal and supportive, and it worked both ways. So, I couldn't get my head around this disinterest.

I tentatively brought it up to try and understand: How come, in the land of who-you-know-not-what-you-know, did not one of his well-connected and employed friends stick their neck out to help him? His response was bitter. Yes, it was true he had many friends with their own businesses, and he also knew plenty of people who worked in specific areas he had always been interested in: fashion, retail and design, not to mention cinema and TV. Sadly, it was every man for himself and, fearful their own positions could become tenuous if they stuck their necks out, they didn't. It was that simple. He had tried several times, but even manual work at exhibitions had proved to be a nightmare as the pitiful amount of money he had earned then had to be chased down.

I remembered the scene of our first argument at Milan airport and blushed. His lack of money had been down to some tight-fisted so-called *friend*.

He continued in the same vein – all of them had connections, money and guaranteed properties left to them by their parents, not to mention the general support offered by close family networks. This was in stark contrast to his own family, who had never made him feel valued, welcomed or included and would happily see him destitute rather than encourage him to leave. His friends were lucky because they didn't have any idea of how hard life was for *real* people. *'Real people like us,'* he would say, hugging me close. *'You are my family now,'* he'd tell me. *'No one else matters, just you and me together from now on.'* I luxuriated in the warmth of his fierce protectiveness. I also recognised his pain and hurt. I had always been considered the black sheep of my own family because of my actions or how I behaved. It had been a standing joke to everyone but me. This was just further confirmation that I had found my life partner. He understood me inside and out because he had felt the same exclusion I had experienced, and I was focused and determined to make sure that there would be no more suffering.

For either of us.

Chapter 14

Doggone!

He had the most beautiful brindle Neapolitan Mastiff called Kevin living at his place at the beach; therefore, I set about looking for a place for the three of us.

I had never owned a dog, so I had no clue what it was like to keep one, what they ate, or what they required in terms of space and exercise. The only two things I did know were **a)** it would be difficult to rent an apartment in England with a 55-kilo dog and **b)** having owned cats, I knew that any visit to the vet in the UK was likely to be exorbitant. Those two facts scared me because I was earning barely enough to cover living expenses for two, but they came as a package, and I liked Kevin. Now, finding something suitable and affordable for the three of us narrowed down my choices, but I was determined.

He taught me a lot about being a pet owner, and as I had no experience, I accepted that he knew best. The fact he would leave that beautiful animal alone in his yard while he came to visit me for several days at a time certainly troubled me, but he brushed off my concerns, reassuring me a friend would be feeding and checking on Kevin's water while he was away. When I asked if he was also taking Kevin out, he hesitated but again blew away my concerns with his breezy knowledge of canines and how they should be treated. '*Dogs are supposed to be kept outside,*' he said. '*You don't have a dog, do you?*' He would smile wryly at me. True enough, when I stayed there, Kevin had barely been allowed inside; even when it rained, he was put in the back of the large car for the night. I wouldn't say I liked or agreed with it, but I didn't know any better and any reservations were dismissed as I was gently chastised for being overly sentimental.

I grew to love Kevin. He was gorgeous and friendly and very protective of me. I would do stupid little dance moves in the tiny courtyard where he was kept, and delighted at the attention, he would jump around mimicking me. It was adorable, and I started bringing him little gifts too: dog treats and squeaky toys, stuff to play with to demonstrate how much I loved him. He was excited when I came to visit due in no small amount to the time I dedicated to playing with him. Too big for me to take out alone, I figured I would become more confident as I became used to his size. He was undoubtedly big and wore an aggressive-looking, thick, studded leather collar giving the impression that he would take a bite out of you as soon as look at you. I hated that collar; it made me feel uncomfortable, giving out the wrong message about Kevin's character which was docile and loving. He, however, laughed at the fear this powerful dog invoked, smilingly telling people that he was harmless and very friendly despite his perceived demeanour. I could tell how much he loved Kevin as he walked tall and proudly, strutting around the town and on the beach with him. There was one thing I was certain of: anyone who loved animals this much was a keeper.

As if everything was conspiring to create the best ending ever for us, after an interminable search, I finally found the perfect place, barely believing my good fortune. It was ideal – spacious, affordable and located in a private park. The entire flat needed a coat of paint, and we would need to start from scratch in terms of furnishings, but this was also a huge positive—no worry of damage or losing the deposit, and the landlord had no issue with pets. Fate really was giving us a helping hand so we could all be together. We would move in and then sort out the logistics of bringing Kevin over. In the meantime, we could leave him with friends.

Then, out of the blue, came the shocker.

I had excitedly called him and breathlessly described the new apartment, perfect for us and our dog, with a private entrance and situated in endless parkland and woods, but he was strangely quiet. My excitement quickly dissipated as he flatly told me the dog had been taken care of. *Taken care of?* The so-called friend who had agreed to look after Kevin for a while had decided to keep him permanently. I demanded to know what the hell had happened. Apparently, this friend had turned up to take the dog away and told him it would be for good, reneging on their agreement to look after him just for a few weeks. He had been left with no choice and hadn't even had time to say goodbye. I was speechless. He adored that dog. What kind of a human being would do that to a friend? I was shocked and disgusted.

He refused to discuss it further, saying the dog had gone to a better place. *'It needed to happen this way,'* he said. Despite my protestations, he would not elaborate or be drawn further; instead, he buried his pain stoically. It was a severe blow, underlining his loathing of Italy and the way people there behaved. Resigned to the loss of his pet, he looked forward to a new life with me in a new country. I didn't say anything more about it because it was too upsetting. Months later, he told me that he had heard that Kevin was happy and had even won prizes in shows. On hearing this, I wanted us to try and find out where he was and maybe visit him to make sure he was OK, but he refused point blank to entertain such a thought; it would be far too painful.

The guilt I felt was unreal.

Chapter 15

Teamwork

It felt like a dream come true.

The endless stream of flights, of bookings and airports, of sad goodbyes and long absences, was finally over.

Strolling through arrivals that last time, wheeling his case, he practically skipped towards me with overwhelming joy. In the same way we had delightedly held onto each other at that first reunion in Rome, we left Gatwick Airport holding hands and laughing at how much our lives had changed in the space of a year. The impatience and frustration we had sometimes felt had been replaced by the knowledge of a permanent and exciting life together under the same roof.

I couldn't wait to start because it felt entirely different from the last time I had tried to share my life with someone. This time, we were working together rather than against each other, and there were no recriminations for anything lacking, not on his side or mine. It felt like we were there for each other, wanting each other to do well, to be better—a direct contrast to how I had felt during my previous marriage, on so many levels. In debt from university, which had taken many years of my working life to pay off, my paltry salaries working in middle management were no match for the six-figure sums my ex-husband had been earning. The ultimate failing had been my infertility. I couldn't even have a baby. In the words of his very expensive barrister, *I didn't deserve anything*.

Now I was with someone so beautiful inside and out, with a clean slate, a new start. I wanted us to be on the same page, and in a faltering-but-trying-to-be-brave voice, I told him that it might not be impossible, but it was highly unlikely we could have children. I gave him a choice. I told him he needed to think long and hard about that because if he did want them, he still had plenty of time to find someone much younger who could do that with ease. Holding my breath as I waited for his answer, he smiled at me lovingly, holding me close, softly reassuring me with the most magical words I had ever heard: '*More time for us!*'

* * *

Our apartment needed an entire overhaul on a shoestring, but undaunted, we set about creating our home. I knew the right places and websites to source second-hand furniture and appliances, and with his style nous, we knew we were a winning team. Gradually, the apartment took shape. While I worked, he gave everywhere a coat of paint, with me helping at weekends. It was ours to do what we wanted, and as a blank canvas, it was perfect. Previously used as accommodation for the grooms at the old stables, all the rooms were huge and spacious. A closed-up connecting door meant there was a large six-foot door-sized gap in the living room to be filled. Anything we put in there was the wrong shape or too small or looked odd, until one day, while looking at it, I had a brainwave: books! Second-hand books would fill it with colour and be a cheap and original way to close it up. We started collecting them from everyone I knew, eventually filling up the gap, and the result was an eye-catching piece of homemade art costing very little. I was over the moon at how it looked.

Naturally, everyone assumed it was down to the stylish and very talented Italian, and they applauded and complimented his abilities and flair for interior design.

How lucky was I to have so much talent available? I didn't correct them, neither did he, although a mild flash of irritation passed through me as I listened to the plaudits he received for it. I was very proud of how it had turned out, but saying it was me would come across as mean and petulant. The chance that somebody liking it might create an opportunity for *him* meant it was unimportant who received the praise.

I knew how lucky I was with his fashion sense as he took such an interest in my clothes and how I dressed. Having spent the last few years living in the T-shirts I regularly stocked up on when in Nicaragua, I had my own idea of what suited me: fitted and long and easy to wash, I wore the T-shirts with jeans, a staple uniform and I was convinced they were perfect. With a slightly disapproving shake of his head, he directed me to other, more feminine tops and away from my bright comfortable favorites. He didn't use the word 'cheap' because I pointed out their branded labels, proving they were good quality. Instead, he smiled sweetly at my naivety, scrunched up his nose and gently told me he was pretty sure they were fake. Feeling faintly ridiculous, I listened to his recommendations about which jeans, tops and shoes I should wear, taking great pleasure when he approved. My friends were both delighted and bemused as I handed over large chunks of my wardrobe to be 'recycled'. '*But you love these,*' they protested. '*Not anymore,*' I laughed, although a tiny part of me did question why I was so intent on getting rid of *all* of them.

I was grateful and happy that things were shaping into a proper relationship. I was constantly putting out feelers for work for him with everyone and anyone. I was frequently reminded by them (and him) that this was a huge upheaval and he needed time to settle in and feel comfortable as well as learn the language and adapt to his new country. Everyone reassured me: *It will happen... just let him relax and enjoy this time together... don't be in a hurry for it all to come together straightaway.*

It was clear I was stressing too much over nothing.

Plus, he was already helping me in one area where I welcomed and appreciated his support—my coffee fairs. For years, I had single-handedly planned, packed up and travelled to various food festivals across the country. The fairs were exhausting, expensive and necessary to build the brand. Wonderful, supportive friends had been fantastic in what could often be a lonely and knackering endeavour. The fairs proved essential for marketing the products. They were also an invaluable lesson in logistical organisation from weighing up the price, location, and size of the stand to the availability of electricity and water. The questions were endless: Would I need more than one coffee machine? Did I have enough promotional material? Had I ordered enough of each roast? Would it be mainly beverage sales or retail? What was the weather forecast? Should I drive back or stay overnight?

No matter how careful I was, I always forgot something vital, and frustratingly, every single item: cups, sugar, coffee jugs, extension leads, business cards were all indispensable, unless, of course, they weren't. One such occasion was turning up to the Brighton Vegan Festival with a carload of milk. While waiting to unload, the initially friendly bearded chap with the clipboard was less than impressed as he opened the back doors to my van. Pointing to the job lot of dairy products stacked up, he declared huffily, *'You won't be bringing those in, will you?'* The penny dropped as I took in the vast array of prohibited items and shook my head. *'Good grief, no!'* I said trying to suppress an embarrassed giggle, but the look on his face told me that veganism is no laughing matter.

Fairs were the backbone of my business, and I loved and dreaded them. The leads could be incredible, or you could fail at the first hurdle. I always had that pressure, and despite my wonderful patient and hard-working friends, the bottom line was me alone.

Until I wasn't.

Suddenly, my knight in shining armour was not only consistently by my side at home, but was now ever-present, sharing my workload. From finding that elusive parking space close enough to easily unload to organising the stand, fetching and carrying water and milk, he was there for whatever was needed, meticulously arranging the packets of coffee in a way to maximise sales while at the same time slapping my hand away if I touched or moved anything on his carefully crafted display. All of which I laughingly accepted because he seemed to know best.

His experience had been as a visual merchandiser, so this was his world. Incorporating design and creativity along with 'playing shop'. He found it stimulating, interesting and different. Appearing totally engaged in this sales-driven customer-facing role, he charmed the customers with his adorable Italian-accented broken English. He regaled, as best he could, the back story of the enterprise that *'his girlfriend had started'*. I made the coffee, smiling happily at him, ecstatic in the knowledge that, after years of coping alone, I had someone permanently by my side to share it all with. I no longer had to scrabble around trying to do it all by myself; I had an actual partner who wanted to make a success out of it just as much as I did. I felt complete. It was a wonderful solution, but it couldn't work long-term. We weren't sharing something we had both created. Instead, it was splitting down the middle my half of something I was already sharing with a northern Nicaraguan community. I felt stuck between loving and appreciating his help and desperately needing him to find his own 'thing', his own source of income. When I brought this up, he was mystified as he certainly wasn't helping me out for money; he was simply trying to do his 'bit' and insisted that anything he 'earned' by helping me out should be put towards our bills.

Can't say fairer than that.

Chapter 16

Mind your language

It was the year of the Summer Olympics and the Diamond Jubilee. The weather may not have ticked all his boxes, but I was determined to show off my country and everything it had to offer. He was here, and I was keen to demonstrate that this was the right place for us to be.

Our relationship was generally a lot of fun, like being in the presence of a big, exuberant kid who saw everything with an air of innocence and surprise. We had in-jokes, even a secret language and stupid noises which made us fall about laughing. We played 'hide and terrify', or at least I did, finding obscure places at home to disappear and then jump out and scare the wits out of him. He was my best friend and soulmate all rolled into one, so when I introduced him to my family, I hoped that they would recognise his qualities and understand that this was the right person for me after all my heartache. It didn't exactly go to plan. They weren't anything other than very nice to him, but I knew their polite manner was non-committal, and my mother was positively tight-lipped. Naturally disappointed, I also understood their guarded reactions; they wanted to make sure I was being looked after properly, and his precarious (non) work status and reliance on me didn't help. Their scepticism motivated me to convince them that this was perfect and *prove* I knew what I was doing.

Our social life was busy, at least initially. Everyone was enthusiastically eager to meet him, and I wanted nothing more than his integration, to see him socialise and practise his English and create those all-important contacts for potential work opportunities. I wanted him to fit in and feel a part of it all. Wherever we went, he was adored and spoilt, and for the most part, they fell for him in the same way I had. His persona was loving, gentle and kind; his good looks and affable nature all helped everyone feel at ease around this laid-back and funny man, who was comical too with his efforts to understand the language. I tried to help him by gently correcting his words and reminding him to use different tenses to make his storytelling clearer so people would understand him more. At least, in my head, that was what I was doing. His pained expression told me how wrong I was. Sighing at my interruptions because, once again, I had put him off his train of thought, he explained to everyone how my endless corrections blocked him, making him too embarrassed to try again. Squidging up his nose, he looked downcast, seemingly saddened by his inability to be allowed to learn slowly. I was gently reprimanded by a chorus of '*Leave him alone*' from people I loved and respected. They understood my intentions, but I was admonished for being a teeny bit overbearing and bossy. '*Let him learn at his own pace,*' they said, smiling at me, and I'd wonder what was wrong with me.

Mortified at being accused of being overbearing, I hid the humiliation and embarrassment washing over me. Maybe I was too pushy; I must be as they had all agreed. Surely he wanted to increase his vocabulary? Find other words and use the correct grammar? From an entirely selfish point of view, improving his English could give me a break from constantly translating every single conversation and help him communicate more freely without always relying on me. They had teased me as never being off duty, constantly pressing him to do better. '*These things take time,*' they said. Seeing my face fall, he'd smile, lean over and gently stroke my face. '*I'm only doing my best,*' his caresses said. Everyone in the room melted at his affectionate sign of loving patience, laughing about my inability to leave the classroom tactics at school. *'Once a teacher...'* and I smiled along, pretending I was OK with that, and we'd finish our pudding.

Surrounded by the people I loved the most in what should have been the happiest of circumstances, there was the slightest, barely perceptible, nagging sensation—like an item of clothing not feeling as comfortable as it used to.

I did understand how hard it was for him. Moving to a new country and learning a language from scratch was something I had done, and it wasn't easy. Learning a language as an adult is seriously hard work, not to mention adapting to an entirely different culture, food, customs and people. I was exceedingly protective if anyone mentioned his lack of English, finding myself becoming impatient when those attempting conversation with him peppered their language with endless colloquialisms, used slang or spoke too fast. Couldn't they see how hard it was for him to follow what they said? He'd look at me pleadingly, and I'd see how lost he was, so I helped, quickly translating to make him feel at ease.

Talk about being stuck between a rock and a hard place. I wanted my friends to make more of an effort so that conversations could be opened up between them and his confidence in speaking would grow. Instead, it backfired spectacularly. Rather than relaxed, free-flowing chats, his disinterest in finding the right words became clear, awkward pauses followed, and it was up to me to translate or fill in the gaps. Losing interest, he either disappeared off somewhere else or disengaged entirely, absorbed with the workings of his phone. Afterwards, he told me it was for my benefit. *'They are your friends, after all,'* he said reasonably, *'I was just leaving you to have time together.'*

Initially, explaining away his lack of progress was simple: a few months is no time at all to adjust. Even after a year, it was acceptable to say he was still new, but as the months passed, it became harder to defend him. I suggested we speak English at home, and we did, until he became tired and refused to participate, preferring his mother tongue. I tried to be understanding and fair. He could understand most of what I said, but it seemed to be a one-way street. His responses were invariably in Italian, and he rolled his eyes at my insistence that we tried for half a day, or a couple of hours, or even twenty minutes to use English. He refused, with the excuse that I was railroading him into something he needed time with. Maybe it was because he had a creative brain, and learning languages wasn't his 'thing'.

The food wasn't his thing, either.

At home, before heading out to see friends, the quizzing would begin about the evening. What would the food be like? Who was making it? His questions would immediately put me on edge, although I couldn't pinpoint why; after all, he was only asking, but somehow, this had created a tiny line of tension about the dinner. Seeing my worry, he'd reassure me and tell me it would all be OK, grinning at me. I then tried to relax; he would be fine, and so would the food. I was overreacting, probably just tired and stressed out from work. I needed to chill. Once we were out, he projected a charm that was disarming for everyone else and somewhat confusing for me. Foods he detested were gobbled up with gusto, and I watched on incredulously as he scooped up peas and carrots as if they were the food of the Gods; the same stuff he would have starved rather than eat if I had served them at home. Noticing my expression of disbelief, he squeezed my hand and winked at me. He was clearly eating them to be polite, but I was still confused – no one would mind if he left them on his plate. If our conversations were overheard, then I had to explain, but, talking over me, he cancelled out what I said and told everyone how deliciously different the vegetables were compared to mine, delighting the hostess and leaving me speechless. I made a note to try them that way at home, but a part of me knew it would be pointless. He willingly tried blue cheese despite having told me more than once how much he loathed it. *'He will never eat that,'* I said, laughing as my friend cut him a wedge and passed it across. As if to prove me wrong, he tried it and asked for more while waxing lyrical about the taste. Everyone fell about laughing, telling me to let him make his own decisions.

It was bewildering, but I figured it was me, not him, because he was definitely trying his best.

Notwithstanding the language barriers and the food issues, I did love being part of a couple. I loved 'us'. We belonged together regardless of any idiosyncrasies; that was part of who we were, and to underline that, he would often try and make me laugh when we were out together. Sometimes, if a joke or story was shared and he was unable to follow, he smiled along with everyone else, pretending he understood. Then he'd whisper to me in Italian – sometimes, it was an innocent comment, but more often than not, it was derisory, something to catch me off guard and make me laugh out loud. Then, when everyone looked to me for an explanation for this unexpected mirth, I had to think quickly to cover whatever he had said.

The social evenings I had always loved so much were changing. No longer relaxing, they felt edgy, as I spent them watchful and worried. Was he OK? Did he like the food? Did he understand everything? Was he bored?

It was bloody exhausting.

Chapter 17

Ten Out Of Ten

I've always been the one to arrange surprise birthdays, special cakes, dinners out and weekends away. A unique present for someone special? I'd find it. Being labelled feisty, go-getting, independent and focused was a compliment; when it came to it, I was more than capable of problem-solving, planning and finding a way. I just didn't want to *always have to do it*. My dream was to be looked after, for someone else to make the decisions, big or small. I wanted to be mollycoddled and spoilt, but above all, I wanted to change the overriding feeling that if something needed to be done, I would have to do it, or it wouldn't happen.

Meanwhile, you couldn't find me under the mountain of CVs and job applications I was buried under to ensure he would find the opening he wanted. I believed, in a way, that was limpet-like to all and everyone that he would find a job, one that suited him down to the ground and that my financial responsibilities would be halved. I would find the security I craved and lusted after.

Yes, lusted after, because I wanted normality, and as far as I was concerned, that came in the form of a boyfriend who provided for us both and who was out all day working to do that. Someone who worried and hoped and wanted the same shit I did, someone who was so tired when he came back from work each day that I would make it my goal to rip his clothes off and make him feel that the exhausting slog was totally worthwhile because, at the end of it, he came home to the best girlfriend ever. The one who, when he walked in the door, made him feel like he was the most important person in her world because there she was cooking the most delicious meal and, oh my god, she's wearing...

No, I am not trying to recreate a 1950s housewife scenario here. I am fully up to date with the concept of emancipation. I believe in sharing—work, money, bills, household chores and sex. It should be fun and interesting, and it takes two to take it in turn at being spontaneous and loving and, well, dirty, I suppose. Just because I work does not mean I am averse to a welcome home in sexy underwear while I have a lasagne in the oven. Unfortunately, the element of surprise dwindles somewhat when it is just one of you taking on *all* the different roles.

Feeling under pressure somewhat lessens that determination to spice things up, and everything very much depended on me – my country, my shoulders. I had promised he would love it here, and I was convinced he would find a wonderful job that would use his talents. I was nothing if not optimistic because I knew he had so much to offer, believing anyone would be lucky to have him. I just needed to find the perfect position and match him up. Doubling my efforts, I made sure he found odd jobs wherever possible, work experience, anything I believed might extend his skillset. It was 2013, and he had been here for two years; whatever had eluded us until now was surely just around the corner.

I never delved into why nothing ever lasted with the few jobs he did try out, or why he was never asked back. I put it down to a lack of extra work or no cash for that extra pair of hands. With each dead-end, I felt he had been let down, but I also felt it personally. It wasn't fair on him when he had so much to offer.

I sounded like a broken record.

I kicked any doubts and insecurities into touch and concentrated on alternative ways of making extra cash to support us through this rough patch. As well as the business, I was offered a part-time teaching job. The school and the kids were great, but I didn't feel confident. They offered me more classes, and I couldn't refuse; we needed the money. I also found house-sitting work and even signed up for dog-sitting jobs, partly for the money but also for him, as I knew how much he missed having his own dog. If I could put in the practice and learn about dogs by looking after them, I would be more prepared when it came to having one of our own.

I managed it all because, as he frequently reminded me, *'You are so good at doing all of that.'*

Chapter 18

Trouble in Paradise

'When we were good, we were very, very good...'

Nothing felt normal, whatever normal is. I was doing everything I could to make our lives the best they could be, and yet, despite a beautiful home and constant searching for job opportunities with as many fillers of good times in between, my best efforts never quite hit the mark.

He wasn't keen on television unless it was *Storage Wars* or a design programme and worried he couldn't share in the downtime I regarded mindless TV to be I came across something he didn't even know he could love—books. I introduced him to reading. He admitted that he had always considered books to be boring and had never really understood the attraction. Encouraged by his interest in what I was reading, I bought him a crime fiction story I figured would appeal, and suddenly, he was hooked. I was enthralled by his enthusiasm and thought it was a crime in itself that he had missed out on so much, so I looked for writers in genres he expressed interest in, mainly corruption and murder mystery by American or English authors, and always in Italian because reading in English would not have been relaxing at all. He adored John Grisham, and it became my mission to find as many titles as possible. I secretly ordered second-hand books and left them in hiding places around the apartment for him to find. He'd slow his reading towards the end of each book, afraid of not having another, unaware that I was already planning a small treasure hunt around finding the next one. Giving something like that, which was relatively small, gave me so much pleasure, but knowing how much he loved it and seeing his sheer joy at discovering another unexpected book was priceless. He became a big, happy kid, dancing around the flat, holding onto his new prize, tickled pink at the surprise, and I would be reminded once again how lucky I was to have him.

We had painted a long blackboard on the wall in the kitchen to write lists and silly messages on. His 'gifts' to me were his very creative drawings, which I would find when I opened the door to the office and came out into the kitchen to make a cup of tea, making me feel very special that I had been on his mind, creating a romantic or funny sketch just for me. He had a natural talent, and many of our friends suggested selling his drawings as a commercial enterprise. He agreed, delighted at the attention and praise. I also agreed, but I didn't have the time to set it in motion.

I was up to my eyes trying to make my business work. My business partner had been true to his word regarding financial help in rebranding the coffee. But when it came down to it, what I desperately needed was a way forward in how to manage the accounts in order to create a better and more viable profitable success. He didn't seem to have the time or resources to help me, and I was drowning in paperwork. An accounts software package I had been advised to buy, which would have worked for a company with 200 staff, was unsuitable for my little cottage industry. I wasn't just scared, I was terrified of letting everyone down, disappearing into the office/dining room, emerging hours later tired, irritable and anxious. In that 'office', I wasn't just looking for leads, contracts and ways to make the coffee company work, but I was also juggling our personal finances to find ways of paying the bills, rent and support our lifestyle, in between sending out his CV.

The stress which ran through me was inevitably having a negative effect on us. He mentioned on more than one occasion that I was difficult to be around and also noted that I wasn't a morning person. In fact, I could be really unpleasant even with the cup of tea he religiously made me. He said he found this 'moodiness' to be very challenging because in his words, *'I always wake up cheerful but you are so cross and you bring me down.'* Appalled at how selfish and obsessed I had been with work when he was clearly doing his best to be positive, I made up my mind to do better. To compensate, I spent time planning lots of interesting things we could do together, things he missed and loved, like visiting different shops or driving to the sea for our favourite lunch treat of fried calamari and chips with a glass of wine. Satisfied we were doing something enjoyable together, he reminded me, *'You need time off too. You deserve it.'* Feeling grateful and relieved, I was able to continue working guilt-free.

I tried to make sure we visited Italy as much as we could, knowing how much he missed the food and the weather, and although he wasn't as keen, it felt important to visit his family too. Dismissing the idea of bringing gifts to a bunch of people who had never bothered with him felt strange to me and in direct contrast to the stunning food parcels of olive oil and hunks of parmesan cheese they sometimes sent us. *'A shouty bunch of crazies,'* he sourly described them. If and when we did visit them, he was itching to leave from the moment we stepped in the door.

Planning our time away was a source of nervous excitement for me as I kept an eye out for cheap tickets and was thrilled when I found suitable deals, meaning we could afford to escape for a few days to his home country. Like a kid at Christmas and full of delight at the prospect of the trip, I surprised him with the news, waiting expectantly for his happy reaction. Chewing his lip thoughtfully, he stared at me, firing questions in quick succession: *What time are we flying? From which airport? What time do we arrive?* As I enthusiastically filled him in on the logistics, he silently counted on his fingers, looking for all the world as if he was solving a complex maths equation.

Then he spoke: *'So we land just after lunch, add an hour for Italy, time to travel to that place takes three hours, so that is one day less'* or *'We have to be up early to catch that 7 a.m. flight, so we will be tired all day, can't include that day'.* Then: *'We will need to spend all day cleaning the property before we leave, discounting the last day as well.'*

With a sinking heart, I tried persuading him that even the travel part would be fun, but raising his eyebrows, he looked at me as if I had flown in from an alternative universe. *'You do realise, at that time of day, it will take ME hours to drive from A to B.'* Huge failing on my part for not considering the journey, traffic in Rome, time to travel to the airport or the beach.

Somehow, no matter what I booked or whatever I arranged, it was never quite right. Any break away together should have been fantastic, and yet, I couldn't suppress the feeling that instead, I was responsible for the curtailing of a good time and missed opportunities through bad planning – he was right, I hadn't considered all the elements for the perfect trip. *'Maybe the next time, you could ask me, and we will look at it together instead of you doing it all,'* he told me, then laughing, he added, *'Impossible! We know you like to be in control of everything'.*

Was that it? Did I? Was I some sort of *control freak?*

Feeling shocked, I questioned myself and my motives. True enough, I earned the money and was very aware of what we could and couldn't afford, but that was not my choice. I would have preferred to hand over the responsibility and not deal with everything, but he refused; it was my country, and therefore, I understood the banking, and he liked how I managed things. Having always admired his nonchalance towards money, I found myself in a hole I had been digging for a long time. He frequently told me he had no idea why people were so fixated on having large quantities of money - he loved the simple things in life, he didn't need much, proudly stating, *'I have never been in debt.'* He didn't even carry a wallet, not liking the look or the feel of it in his pocket.

I kept everything, from cash to all the bank cards, and managed everything coming in and going out. On more than one occasion, I mislaid a bank card and, dissolving into a blind panic, I'd trawl through paperwork and coat pockets looking for it, worrying myself stupid about how we would manage without it while simultaneously praying to Saint Anthony, the patron saint of lost causes. I'd look up to see him leaning against the door, grinning at me, spinning the missing card he had found between his fingers. 'What **are** we going to do with you?' he'd ask.

'When we were good, it was very, very good, but when we were bad... it was horrid.'

Spending money added a jarring note of worry to my already busy head, which in turn activated a vicious cycle of guilt with an obvious outcome: spending = worry = stress = argument, followed inevitably by remorse. And repeat. I was concerned that things weren't progressing at all; in fact, they seemed to have ground to a halt altogether. His language skills were adequate and yet there were no job offers, no callbacks and no interviews. Nothing. Even worse, he seemed less than bothered. Feeling very much alone at having to keep everything afloat, I was finding it hard to keep a lid on my resentment:

'Why can't you find work?'

'Why is it so hard to find something? Anything?'

'What is wrong with you?'

Questions he didn't have the answers to were not up for discussion. Staring at me in silence while chewing his lip, daring me to continue, I could feel my temper rising. The one question guaranteed a response, the one he truly hated was:

'Where is your bloody initiative?'

This I yelled, frustrated beyond belief at his total lack of drive or enterprise. At that point, all hell would break loose.

Perhaps because the other questions could be blamed on circumstance or language issues or the lack of opportunity, but that one question put the blame firmly on his shoulders. His stock answer was to turn it back around on me: *'I'm here, aren't I? I am trying everything I can. If you have all the answers and are so clever, what do YOU think I should do, seeing as this is your country?'*

My throat would close up in a knot of hopelessness because I had nothing left to say. Why didn't I have all the answers? Something inside me pushed through and raged back:

'This is not *all on me. You are a grown man, and you have to take some responsibility.'*

On realising I was not going to let it go, his fury became almost physical, rearing up, all six foot six of him, a boiling mass of anger, he shouted back, sneering and vicious as he told me exactly what was wrong with me:

'You pick and pick and pick until I cannot stand it anymore,' he said nastily. *'You can't help yourself, can you? Happy when you have pushed the calmest, most patient person to the very edge. You love arguing, it makes you feel alive, and you pick and spit your poison until I retaliate because that's what you really want, and you don't stop till you succeed in driving me insane. This is the real you, shouting and screaming at me, saying vile things until I can't take it anymore, and I have to respond. You make me argue back, and that is not who I am, it is who* **you** *are.'*

He continued in the same vein, holding his head with both hands, screaming at me to stop. He walked purposefully towards an open window, and in the loudest voice in perfect English, he shouted, *'Leave me alone,'* at the top of his voice. Seeing my shocked face, he continued in Italian, swearing and moaning and groaning that he couldn't stand it anymore, punching a door or a wall, pleading with me to stop. *'Look what you have done to me,'* he'd yell. *'Are you finally happy now I am in this state?'*

I watched in silent disbelief. I had no idea who this hysterical person was, I didn't recognize anything about him. The idea that my questions had led to this dramatic and uncontrollable reaction left me feeling exhausted and emotionally spent. With no resolution between us, I wondered if I really was the sort of person who was only happy when making someone I loved miserable. I was evidently unable to resolve this in a calm and reasonable manner. I had an unmanageable temper I had been unaware of, and it was frightening both of us.

Who the hell was I turning into?

On one occasion, we had gone for a walk in the surrounding fields on a beautiful sunny day. For some reason, we argued, something to do with lack of work or money. I cannot recall exactly, but I remember it escalated quickly, becoming heated and unpleasant. Looking at me with a vaguely triumphant expression, he said softly, *'Now I understand what they mean.'* I whipped my head around to look at him, and he continued, *'I didn't believe it, but I can see it now.'*

'Who?' I asked in total shock. *'What did who say?'*

'Your closest friends,' he calmly replied. *'They all say the same thing.'* Smiling sadly, he carried on. *'They told me to accept it because it's who you are.'* He shrugged, watching me closely, well aware of the impact his words were having on me.

The pain and hurt I felt inside was something I couldn't believe, let alone control. That people I loved and trusted were talking about me *to him*, discussing my flaws, damning my personality, it was so horrendous and unbelievable, so horrible that I felt he had to be lying, but that didn't make any sense. The anger flooded through me. I slapped him. In the middle of that field, with tears in my eyes, I slapped his face.

I stood still, shaking and trembling, horrified at my outburst. Holding his face, he looked at me, and seeing my remorse, he reached out to hug me.

The fact he was so forgiving was a relief and evidence of what an incredibly understanding and compassionate man he was. I am not that person I told him over and over. I am so, so sorry. I clung to him, feeling both shame and disgust. How could I have done that? Why did I do that? He was so loving, holding me gently, allowing me to take his hand and to kiss his face. His pained and hurt but soft expression made me feel even worse, especially when he said that he understood how much pressure I was under. I promised I would make it up to him, and he reassured me that the work situation was short-term and would be resolved. In light of what had just happened, his employment situation seemed trite and unimportant, relegated to the back seat. What truly mattered was us.

He was here, wasn't he? He had moved countries for us. All he wanted was the girl I was when he met me. Overcome with guilt, I realised how true this was. He had done everything for us to be together, and I was so grateful. I needed to be that girl again, not the horror story of a woman I had become. I had to mind my temper and be patient; he had suffered quite enough with his own family. I needed to show him that I was the epitome of stability and safety and make everything work.

I confided in friends about our arguments, and they batted away my concerns. *'Of course, things were going to be fiery!'* they claimed. *'The combination of your Irish temper and his Mediterranean passion was bound to create fireworks.'* They grinned at me, and the implication was clear. I was lucky. *We* were lucky because it was a heady combination of intense passionate nationalities. Listening to their encouraging words, I felt the same sensation of helplessness sweep over me. I couldn't explain why I was so worried because, as far as they were concerned, I had struck romantic gold; he was incredible, and I was worrying too much. So what if there were rows? Everyone had those. Didn't that follow with some amazing making up? I was regarded fondly by these people whose only wish was to see me happy.

I nodded in agreement, lying through my smiling teeth, once again losing the power to formulate the words which would have told them an entirely different story.

With one good friend, I felt comfortable enough to be more honest and admitted to her that I was scared of my own temper as my rage had reached the point where I had lashed out physically. Her reaction was extreme shock. '*That is* NOT *acceptable, you need to control that,*' she said, almost coldly. Verbal nastiness she could understand, but physically losing it with someone was abuse, whether it was male or female—no grey areas. I listened to her, tears prickling my eyes, my face burning. I lowered my head in shame.

Even worse, I realised I wasn't that different from the ex-boyfriend who had used his fists so freely on me.

I really was the pits of a human being.

Chapter 19

The Great Pretender

Fake it till you make it.

Don't we all do this at some point in our lives? In school, during tests or exams, at interviews, or even in a sports match.

I played for a work netball team, never believing I was any good. I just turned up each week for the laughs and the exercise. The coach totally rated me. Encouraging and motivating all of us, she put us forward for an inter-office match. Her cool, calm demeanour was incredible—she believed in us. We slayed the opposition after I scored fifteen times. A lifetime of being told I was clumsy, and we won. Nearly twenty years later, I still remember every minute.

Sometimes, you just want to be given the opportunity—the chance to show how good you are, even if you have doubts. I've done this throughout my career, and I know I am not alone. We are full of bluster, demonstrating a shiny veneer of a 'can do' attitude, while the Sunday Night School Nerves practise somersaults with the butterflies in our stomachs.

During my first marriage, I was given a job as facilities manager in an engineering company with a great salary and benefits. (Hang on! It wasn't *'given to me'*. I applied and was successful). After signing the contract, my confidence started to seep away, and imposter syndrome set in because I knew I didn't really have a clue how to do the job. In those scary first few weeks, I went in every single day with a large bottle of water, and on the recommendation of a good friend, I added drops of Rescue Remedy to calm me down, and somehow, it worked. I encountered a ton of hostility from diehard staff members unwilling to change the old systems, who knew best because their own experience mattered more. The same ones who spent their days smiling to my face but whose animosity was obvious because I had been given a role that changed theirs. Each day I went in, and in the face of those office politics, I faked knowledge and ability big style—I wasn't going anywhere, so I needed to convince them, and they needed to accept me—which they did. Eventually.

It helped that I had managed to create my own loyal and wonderful admin team. I had their backs, and they had mine because I defended, praised and supported them all. It turns out I *was* cut out for that job, and my strengths lay in building up the confidence of the people who had none. It became *my thing* and made me a good people manager in all sorts of areas. It compelled me to work hard at creating funds for the coffee-growing communities in Nicaragua, the farmers who had very little. I was determined to show them what they did have and make the most of it, changing things for the better but always with a prevailing sense of fairness, whether it was a farming family in the community who needed more or a shy secretary who was looking for a promotion.

* * *

Back in my own life, we did a brilliant job of pretending to all and sundry that he was living the dream despite the many obstacles we faced. That fakery extended to a much wider audience when I created a Facebook account for him. Despite his protestations that he was not interested in modern technology, he quickly became addicted to the 'likes' on photos he posted. His increasing number of 'friends' validated all aspects of his life and, by proxy, mine.

Social media has a lot to answer for in our need to feign an enviable lifestyle. Stuck in traffic? Look how empty the roads are here in this video. You live in a city? Check out the beautiful countryside and trees here. Living in a high rise? Look at the town we live in, with original Tudor buildings. So quaint. And on and on it goes. Look at me, and what a great time I'm having. I have photos and videos to prove how thin, happy, tanned or in love I am. But what if we aren't? What happens if that photo shows that you have turned into a bit of a fatty-fat-fat or, heaven forbid, you can see wrinkles, crow's feet or an expanding waistline? Then what? This pretence is leading (who am I kidding?) *has already* led to so much damage in terms of how we see ourselves and how others see us—it's all a pack of glossy fibs.

In the olden days when we were out with friends, and someone had a camera (an actual camera), we were lucky to all be in the frame at the same time, never mind finding the right position to pout, show off your best side and then edit the picture according to how you want to be seen. When those grainy, faded, colour photos were developed, it was enough to have been there in that moment, even if half of your body was out of shot. It's joyful to look back now and see how young we were and how ridiculous our hair, expressions and taste in clothes were—at best odd and at worst embarrassing. Nowadays, in a world of fabrication and deceit, we actively hunt down authenticity and spontaneity, which, weirdly, we used to have but felt we should improve. Until it disappeared.

Passing yourself off as perfect, regardless of whether you are or not, is a risky strategy. Deep down, a part of you knows it isn't right, and if something inside of you is unwilling to go along with that deception, then you are holding onto a ticking bomb.

Chapter 20

The Trying Game

I had a busy year in 2013.

I needed to repay the business loan and find a way to make the enterprise more successful, so most of my days were spent glued to my laptop in the dining room/home office. Finding lucrative fairs to connect me to leads meant potential long-term contracts, and then I could demonstrate to my business partner that I was capable. An incredibly successful businessman, he was sneeringly dismissive of my efforts, and I was more than a little scared of him but equally determined to find a way. I did everything possible, and through sheer effort, I negotiated a deal with a local hotel group. This was excellent news, but my business 'partner' remained unconvinced and refused to back it. In the end, I was approached by an angel of a friend. Believing in me, the coffee company and the potential of this contract, she lent me the money, and I felt as if I had been given a lifeline.

The Italian, meanwhile, was working at various interim odd jobs. Helping out with some painting at the local pub was OK, but they desperately needed a bar manager. They felt his good looks and gregarious charm would be perfect, but his language skills let him down. He agreed it was a pity, but if people didn't speak clearly, how could *he* be expected to understand a word of it? I was disappointed, as it would have been the ideal opportunity. '*I have no problem understanding English when you speak to me, unlike those bacon eaters,*' he said, eyes sparkling in merriment as he mimicked their voices, underlining his impossible predicament and trying to make me laugh at the absurdity of it all.

He mocked people he considered beneath him, including those who were too pale, too fat, wore terrible shoes or dull clothes. He had precious little time for any of them and didn't waste his energy on trying to understand what they were saying. Sighing, I agreed it would be unfair of me to expect him to accept a role he would be unable to do properly. Instead, the pub offered me some waitressing shifts, which I gratefully accepted.

We stumbled through the year with some extra cash coming in from his small property in Italy. This converted garage used to be a part of the main villa but had been split off and sold separately. Bought for him by his dad, they had turned it into a place he could stay rent-free. Adding a pre-fabricated wooden shed to one side of the garage created a makeshift kitchen and a small bathroom. With the perfectly sized courtyard and the incredible location by the beach, I recognised its potential as a holiday let as soon as I saw it. Not used to the concept or even the possibility of his very basic space being a rentable property, he took some convincing, but I knew what I was doing, I had experience of this type of work already, and with its proximity to the beach and the city of Rome and with some TLC on the inside, I knew it could be remarkable.

Every holiday was spent repairing, cleaning, painting and updating the property, adding items we had bought in England to improve it and make it more homely and attractive for future renters. Decent towels, simple bed covers, cushions and pictures, nautical stuff in line with the location, and slowly but surely, it came together, as did the bookings. Often, it was hard to manage from such a distance but manage it I did: cleaning, reservations, emails and even the complaints. *'Well done,'* he said proudly, *'you are a genius!'* With that crumb of a compliment, I felt it was my duty to carry on. Encouraging him to manage it, I said I could explain the booking procedure, making it his project; however, he declined, citing his lack of computer skills. Besides, I was good at it, so it made more sense for me to maintain it.

He began channelling his creative genius towards upcycling furniture. Long walks on the beach became about picking up pieces of driftwood and making them into little pieces of art, spending hours sanding, painting and waxing tables and chairs. I encouraged it all, proudly talking about his creative side to anyone who would listen. Finally, he was showing off what he was really about, and we planned a summer coffee fair where he had his own stand selling the different pieces he had worked on. It was a moderate success, and once again, I began to anticipate a brighter future.

It was short-lived.

While he loved the accolades and compliments he received for his creations, it wasn't the money-spinner he expected. Undoubtedly a success, but far too much effort for such a small return, and with winter coming, it would be cold outside, and he couldn't be out there preparing furniture in all weathers.

Encouraged by me, he signed up with a recruitment agency and was sporadically called in for kitchen porter work. The pubs and hotels were often in the middle of nowhere with no public transport, so I had to drop him off or pick him up at the end of his shift. In one place, he felt discriminated against, *'probably for being Italian'*. Finding that hard to believe as most kitchen workers were foreigners themselves, I probed him further. *'What do you mean they picked on you? How?'*

When pushed for details, all he could tell me was that he had requested a decent coffee, not the watery instant crap everyone else drank. *'I don't understand why I couldn't have one from the espresso machine, but they told me the kitchen staff weren't allowed to use it.'* He shrugged his shoulders at the insanity of such a petty rule, but seeing my uncomfortable expression, he softened the blow, telling me how he had proudly talked of my coffee company and what I did, and how great THAT coffee was.

I didn't comment but could only imagine the reaction of the others when he made his special beverage request, or turned down the sub-standard instant coffee, or bragged about what he had at home and why. Gritting my teeth, I managed to cheer him up by saying, *'Don't worry, no need to go back there, we will find somewhere else.'* The recruitment agency stopped calling. As the prospect of a job he would enjoy became more elusive, our life, in turn, operated on a swings and roundabouts system, smooth and easy if we had bookings from the place in Italy, money from jobs coming in, fun stuff planned, delicious meals cooked and holidays booked. At these points, I was also the girl he adored, but I had to keep up this life of happiness, ease and joy.

An impossible and unequal task.

The arguments degenerated into nasty personal slanging matches. If I said I couldn't do something because I was busy, then I was addicted to my laptop and preferred being shut off in an office all day. *'You are only happy when you are working, you never want to do anything fun at all,'* he complained. The digs continued: I was always stressed, I never laughed anymore, I was dull or tired or *boring*. I fought back, his stinging comments upsetting me, but unwilling to accept his accusations, I bit back: Without me working how were we supposed to pay for anything? How would we manage to ever go anywhere if there was no money? At these perfectly legitimate points, his reaction would become scornful and derisory; he would groan and throw back his head in exasperation and tell me: *'It's always the same story, here we go again ... money, it is always about bloody money, you are obsessed with money and your need to be in control of everything.'*

Frustration surged through me, making him understand I was doing everything in my power to try and hold it together fell on deaf ears, logical explanations were unwelcome, so loudly talking over me, jeering and sniping, he cut me off, leading me to complain about his inability to find a job and his excuses for not speaking English. Backing himself into the corner of the room where he had gone with his hands up to defend himself in the event of a physical onslaught from me (I would be nowhere near him at this point), I moved away hiding in the bathroom or the office with a door between us for his good and mine.

Changing tack, he followed me. *'Look at what you have become,'* he'd say contemptuously. *'Alone all of the time, that's what you like best – you never wanted a real relationship, incapable of keeping a man, like so many of your friends, you don't know how to have a real relationship, all you want to do is work work work.'* Then, hearing no response from me, he ended with, *'You love starting an argument, spitting your poison, making a person feel bad and then walking away, unable to hear the truth.'*

Eventually, one or both of us would go off somewhere to be alone, exhausted, hurt and reeling from the whole nasty episode, like an animal licking their wounds. I would go back into the office or kitchen to find a glass filled with flowers he had picked from outside, left on my desk with a note, and I would feel so sad at what a nightmare we could be. I'd look for him and find him invariably doing something for me, such as the laundry or tidying up, something to underline how loving and caring he was. Then seeing me he'd open his arms with a sorrowful expression and hold me tightly.

Of course, he didn't mean anything he had said; all he wanted was the girl in me back, the one who wasn't always working. He loved me so much and just wanted a peaceful life with both of us doing whatever it took to make the other one happy. Sometimes, I would try and tell him that I did want him in my life, that it wasn't true I didn't want and need a man. He shushed me, saying, *'We don't mean what we say in arguments, we just say things to hurt the other person in that moment, not because they are true.'*

A. Vicious. Cycle.

To show me how much he loved me, he accepted a job as a part-time kitchen porter in the local pub, not ideal, but perhaps a stepping stone onto something more suitable. I was the eternal optimist.

Chapter 21

Grow up

My mum died.

I have tried to word that differently or find some sort of suitable introduction, but there isn't one. Neither old nor ill, it was unexpected and shocking. Sadly, we didn't have the best relationship, and I am not sure she ever approved of how I lived my life despite my best efforts to make her proud. I didn't match up to her expectations, and my failure to provide her with grandchildren made her – in her own words – feel guilty. Although quite why she took on guilt about my infertility was beyond me, I carried more than enough of it for both of us.

She was taken to hospital, and less than a week later, she was gone.

After receiving the distressing phone call with news of her stroke, I picked him up from his washing-up job, and he drove the two hours to the hospital while I sat crying next to him, a bundle of taught nerves terrified of arriving 'too late'. Staying day and night at the hospital, waiting, hoping and worrying, was a time when all you wanted to do was support your loved ones and be supported by those closest to you. He hung awkwardly around, not knowing what to do or say, and I was torn between irritation and my need to make sure he was OK.

With family gathering from England and Ireland and the 'Hostess with the Mostest' lying seriously ill in a hospital room, the question of where everyone was to sleep was being hastily organised by those who had availability. Reeling from everything that was happening around me, he motioned to me. *'Is there anywhere to maybe get a sandwich or a packet of crisps? Even just a packet of crisps.'* I duly rooted around in my purse, looking for change so he could eat.

I clearly remember my brother's wife disappearing one afternoon. She had popped down to Marks & Spencer's to buy my brother fresh underwear and socks as he had brought none. Hearing that, I went into the toilet cubicle, silently crying my eyes out, my throat closing up in a tight vice-like grip, my usual physical reaction to feelings of total inadequacy. I wasn't crying for my mum, but selfishly for myself, because I also wanted that special someone, aware of the situation, who would wordlessly look after me, appearing with brand new knickers or a snack—something, anything, to help in a small way to make me feel loved and cared for.

After Mum died, I was at the family house trying to pick up the shocked pieces of my dad, who was his usual stoic self, and standing there was my *soulmate,* sticking out like a sore thumb, not knowing what to do or say to anyone. I asked him if he wouldn't mind going back to our place, at least until after the funeral. With so much planning to do, it might be easier on him and he would be needed at the pub. That was when he sort of broke down.

When I say 'sort of', I mean that he looked incredibly sad, and his eyes filled up without spilling over into real tears, although he certainly looked downcast. I thought it was because of my mum and what was happening, and I was shocked, not to mention annoyed with myself, that I hadn't noticed before what an effect all this was having on him. As it turned out, I couldn't have been more wrong.

He couldn't cope with the shifts at the pub because he felt the others in the kitchen were bullying him and laughing at his lack of English, generally not being very friendly, and he was finding it hard to cope. He hadn't wanted to tell me or burden me with this and had tried to keep going but was at his wits end with it all. Plus, he was suffering considerably with dreadful pain in his arm, probably due to a repetitive strain injury from the lever of the washing-up machine. He needed to see a doctor about it.

I wish I was joking.

If there is one surefire way to garner my sympathy, it's someone being bullied in any way, shape or form. I can't bear the injustice of it – the cowardly, sniping way someone takes cheap shots at another person, usually as a result of their own low self-esteem. He knew that already, as it was something we had discussed before. I have had plenty of experience of it at school and in various workplaces. Appalled that anyone would do that to someone so gentle and so lovely, I was adamant he was not to go back there, absolutely not. We would cope without that money and find him something else. I asked him to go back for now and allow me to stay with my dad for a bit, and then I would be back to sort it all out.

Job done. Literally.

* * *

After the funeral, I returned home after reluctantly leaving my dad, who sadly needed time to be on his own. When a parent dies, your inner child suffers. Ironically that childish part needs looking after as if it knows it needs to be grown up but isn't quite ready. It needs cosseting and cuddling until it is strong enough again. I looked for that when I came home, I needed it so badly. Instead, I was greeted by an unemployed man-child who was unable to cope with my grief and had his own needs. With no tender loving care available and a totally depleted immune system, I caught some sort of Dickensian chest infection and was bedridden with pleurisy.

Life was not exactly turning out how I had imagined.

Chapter 22

I do not

I remember that Christmas as clear as jingle bells.

We had decided on a quiet one, just the two of us, with family visiting the following day. Early evening, we sat relaxing, having finished a late dinner in my usual office space, now cleared of all files and paperwork and beautifully decorated with a subtle festive feel and a gorgeous tree in the corner.

'It's been lovely, hasn't it?' I said. *'Despite everything, we have managed to have a lovely day.'*

He smiled back at me, his expression a little odd. *'Do you think it's over?'* he asked, grinning. *'You haven't had all of your presents yet.'*

I didn't understand, and with him refusing to help me by saying any more, I started clearing away the plates. Suddenly, he grabbed my hands, laughing, his eyes darting back and forth, and said, *'There is one more thing…'* I honestly didn't know what he was talking about. I sat back down at the table. *'You need to look for your last present,'* he insisted, and his eyes stared intently at me. Weirdly, they were full of mirth, yet he seemed to have teared up too. He flicked his eyes towards the little Norwegian spruce and back to me again. I looked at the tree and then around the room but couldn't see anything, and then I did—a piece of paper rolled up with a red bow sitting on one of the upper branches.

Retrieving it from its hiding place and returning to the table, there was now a little box by my place setting. Hiding my confusion, I felt my heart sink to my toes, and butterflies stirring in my stomach as my body panicked while silently screaming *NO THANK YOU!* Not now, not like this. My mum had died less than two months before, and I was still in shock over that. We had talked about the *possibility* of marriage, but I sure as shit wasn't in any hurry, nor did I think he was.

Feeling more than a little anxious but putting on my happy, surprised face, I slowly opened the box to find the ugliest ring you could possibly imagine sitting inside.

I could see how much this meant to him as he smiled at me expectantly. His eyes shone with emotion as he talked about the ring. *'It belonged to my mother,'* he said. *'I know it isn't exactly your style, but I wanted to give you something meaningful to celebrate this moment.'* My overriding feeling was one of embarrassment. I knew exactly how he felt about his mother, and it wasn't pretty, and *'not my style'* was an understatement. Aware of my diplomatic shortcomings, I desperately didn't want to put my clunking foot in it; this was not the moment for brutal honesty, so instead, giving the moment the gravitas I could see he felt it was deserving of, I carefully picked up the letter, reading quietly through his flowery handwritten prose, feeling him nervously watching me.

It spoke at length of two hearts coming together from the north and the south of Italy and reuniting despite generational and familial pressures against them. It spoke of a love so strong it would win and outlast everything, romanticizing the idea of two people coming from very different lands to end up together against all odds. It continued, waxing lyrical about his parents' love story and its parallels with our fairytale, explaining it all with tenderness and hope.

I concentrated on every word and, breathing deeply, pretended to be enthralled with the proposal. I told him how much I appreciated the gesture and how much I loved him. *'It's absolutely beautiful that you would do this, but it might be a little soon after my mum and everything. Could we just wait a bit? Maybe not tell everyone just yet?".* Agreeing it was a bit soon and explaining the timing, he said, *'I just wanted to do something wonderful to take your mind off everything. It was only because I love you so much.'* Trying and failing to hide his embarrassment, I soothed my less-than-enthusiastic response with praise over the surprise and how wonderfully romantic he was.

Recovering from the slight awkwardness, he told me he had actually wanted to propose to me with a *flash mob*. Holding my breath, I listened as he described his disappointment at the unwillingness shown by someone he barely knew when he had approached them for help. *'I messaged her, telling her I needed help as I don't know enough people here and I wouldn't even know where to start.'* He added, *'Unfortunately, she never got back to me, which I thought was a bit off. She could have replied.'* I agreed, offering a silent prayer of thanks to this person.

I rarely wore any jewellery, so he suggested a chain so I could wear it around my neck.

'Hmm, maybe,' I said.

It wasn't so much of a refusal, more of a *maybe eventually*. It wasn't about the unfortunate ring, the proposal itself, or the timing. I didn't feel as if it could *never* be right – just not yet. Walking with my dad the following day, I tentatively mentioned the proposal. He looked at me gently and said, *'Bit soon.'* I nodded.

Chapter 23

For Richer, For Poorer

When you see off one dreadful year, the hope is the next is going to be better, be different. Well, 2014 turned out to be all of that and worse...

The biggest change was the amount of time I spent with my dad, regularly driving down to see him, filling his freezer with home-cooked food and teaching him how to make simple meals for himself. He visited more, too, coming up to watch his beloved rugby in the local pub or relaxing at ours, happily listening to Radio 4 and reading *The Telegraph* on his iPad while I happily indulged him with roast dinners and copious amounts of homemade lemon meringue pie.

He was managing on his own, but I knew he found it a struggle, hiding the fact not to cause worry. I loved every second of his company. He was calming and made me feel safe. One day in the summer, after a lovely long lunch, we were chatting over a cup of tea when, out of the blue, he asked me about children. '*Do you still want them?*' he asked, surprising me.

'*Yes,*' I replied. '*I never really stopped, but I had put it to the back of my mind.*' He asked me to investigate it as a real possibility, and if I needed IVF, he would pay for it if it was something we would like to pursue. I had stopped believing this could or would ever be a possibility and being offered the chance to try left me speechless. I hugged my dad tightly, and as he hugged me back, he gruffly said, *'Life is too short not to do what we really want; otherwise, what is it all for?'*

I had no idea if it was even a possibility at my age, but I was thrilled to be given even a tiny window of opportunity. The first step was meeting with an amazing gynaecologist who wasted no time mincing her words. She agreed my age could be a factor, but I was healthy and fit, and she felt it was worth a try. When I happened to mention an intense, sporadic pain I'd experienced in my abdomen area, she made an appointment for a scan so we could go from there.

I was happy, he was happy, and we talked excitedly about baby names, both of us loving the idea of a girl. *'Our own little family,'* he would say over and over. *'Our own sweet tiny family.'* He'd dance around the kitchen. Suddenly, life seemed on the up.

His work was still bitty, and he regularly went out looking for coffee leads or up-cycled a piece of furniture to sell. Interviews weren't forthcoming, but I had my own problems, fully immersed in trying to extricate myself from my business partner.

I was in and out of hospital, poked and prodded to find the cause of my infertility. I soon had my answer: a massive fibroid expanding across my left-hand side, pushing all notions of conception firmly away. I felt disappointment and sadness at so much time wasted and relief, too, at finally understanding the cause of the severe stabbing pains. Also showing up were traces of endometriosis across the top of my uterus, but my clever doctor told me if we removed the fibroid, then that area would be free, and I could possibly conceive. I threw my sadness out because nothing mattered more than to finally be given a chance at the one thing I had longed for my whole life and with him, my soulmate. We had even chosen a name for the baby girl I was now sure we would have.

I came home one day to find him sitting on the bed, looking very serious. Immediately thinking about family, I asked worriedly, *'What's happened?'*

'I have sold my car in Italy,' he said solemnly. This wasn't just good news; it was The. Best. News. Ever.

When I met him, he owned a two-seater sleek American sports car he had bought while working as a visual merchandiser – an expensive, petrol-guzzling Batmobile of a car.

No matter how reluctant he was to let it go, even he understood it wasn't ideal. The trouble was the market wasn't exactly teeming with buyers for that sort of car, and it had to be moved around from one garage to another in the hope of someone buying it – not an easy thing to do when you no longer live in the country. He had called on everyone he knew to move it from place to place; even his dad was involved. I had all but given up hope that it would ever sell, so I was ecstatic. *'That's bloody marvellous news,'* I yelled, jumping all over him.

He wasn't as happy about the low offer he had accepted. *'I should have had at least 8k more,'* he grumbled. *'The buyer was very lucky.'*

I couldn't contain my joy. *'It's gone,'* I said, laughing my head off in relief. *'Not only do we not have to worry about moving it anymore, but we also have 10k in the bank.'*

I danced the dance of joy all around the flat; I felt I could breathe again. We were always scrimping and saving and looking for cheap deals or the most economical ways of doing things, always searching for the best way to save on a few pounds here and there. Everything had always been so difficult, and suddenly, this felt like a lottery win—not life-changing, but enough to pull us up to the top of life's rollercoaster.

Chapter 24

In Sickness and in Health

Finding a lump on my breast was a bit of a bummer.

Before the biopsy results came in, we were off on holiday, so I shoved any bad thoughts to the back of my mind and the two of us headed off to a village in the far south of France where I owned my own place, a house I had bought outright just after returning from Nicaragua following my first year out there.

I had sold the house in the UK and bought one in France: a safety net – my pension – with the thought that one day I could move there and live in it or sell it. But for now, it was money I couldn't spend, tied up in the bricks and mortar that made up this beautiful converted stable tastefully renovated in a contemporary style set over three floors with a spiral staircase connecting them and a private roof terrace where you could sit with a glass of the local wine and watch the sunset over the red-tiled village rooftops. It was hard to imagine a more peaceful and tranquil setting. You had to drive to the coast, but there were plenty of swim spots and rivers nearby, and vineyards graced every hillside.

We didn't often go because his place in Italy always needed so much managing and updating, but this time, with a bit of extra money in the bank, we treated ourselves to a lovely few days in France. Finding the time to cross the border into Spain, we spent a couple of nights in a gorgeous coastal town where he proposed on the terrace steps of a hillside whitewashed church, properly this time. I accepted because the time felt right, happily adjusting the big plastic flower ring he had not so secretly bought earlier in the day. Browsing in the little gift shop that morning, he had picked it up and looking at me with shining eyes, asked, *'You want this one?'* I nodded, smiling shyly because we both knew what it meant.

We headed home, rested, happy and engaged with more hospitals and scans before I started back at school.

As the consultant delivered the bad news, I was more concerned about how he was going to cope with the results. Triple negative stage three breast cancer was worse than I had expected, and, as anticipated, he took it badly, very badly indeed. Swearing a great deal, reffing and blinding about the unfairness of it all, furious with the disease whose name he point blank refused to mention, *'Bloody fuck disease,'* he repeated in almost perfect English, walking around our flat, angrily slamming doors and drawers. I was upset for him, for me and especially for my dad, who took the horrible news in silence before reassuring me over and over in his calm and steady voice that everything would be OK, less than one year after losing his beloved wife.

That same wonderful man who had been through so much grief already in the last twelve months accompanied me to see the consultant about the treatment I would receive. He wanted to be my second pair of ears with so much information to take in. He treated me to lunch at Carluccio's beforehand, and we tried to keep it light and cheery as the sky outside darkened in total contrast. *'A tenner says it's chemo,'* I said, putting the word worse than Voldermort out there. He disagreed but did agree to the bet. *'I feel bad taking your money,'* he said, his eyes twinkling as we headed to the hospital.

It was a lot of information to take in; the tumour had been small, but deep and could cause trouble, *and triple negative* meant an intense type of chemo to make sure it was gone for good, taking with it all my hair, a great deal of my immune system and any teeny tiny chance I would now ever have of conceiving. I looked at my dad, who was looking at me, making himself smile and trying so hard to hold back his own tears. Grinning, I said, *'You owe me a tenner.'* I have two main coping mechanisms when things are tough: retail therapy, or in the event a pretty item of clothing won't suffice, a dark and somewhat inappropriate sense of humour. Discovering I was in for the whole shebang of chemotherapy and radiotherapy, I duly started planning unsuitable headgear and regaling close friends with stories of the reaction to my diagnosis. *'Apparently, if you can choose a cancer, breast is best,'* I told them wryly, and we fell about laughing and crying at the crap you had to deal with in life. He, on the other hand, didn't understand how I could be so blasé about the whole thing, how I refused to be angry or upset that I had *'this, this thing'* as he referred to it, barely able to articulate what was happening. Trying to put myself in his position, I took his hand, calmly explaining to him how much I needed him not to be afraid and how we should just tackle it head on. *'It's not fair,'* he moaned. *'Why did this have to happen to us?'* It seemed strange to me, the idea of wallowing; I couldn't do that, couldn't think about the *why* behind it, not when we needed to be practical. Trying to find something to blame, he told me, *'We need to change your diet. You need vitamins, less sugar, more sun and less stress.'* I agreed to it all while wondering how exactly we were going to achieve that.

I'm a shit patient. I hate being incapacitated, and I especially do not want to be a burden on anyone. My friends, far and wide, built up an invisible support wall around me and made me feel stronger and more able to cope. Sending gifts of healthy recipe cookery books, vitamins and creams, some even clubbed together to surprise me with a fancy machine I could easily make immune system-boosting drinks with. He was incredibly sweet, packing me little lunchboxes full of healthy snacks so I would always have something while teaching. When I came home, he checked to make sure they were empty and would smile approvingly. I'd find lovely drawings on the kitchen board demonstrating how strong I was being and how proud of me he was. I would share them on social media so everyone we knew could see just how much he was doing for me. What an amazing, supportive boyfriend.

He had been busy spending weeks trawling the internet, looking for his ideal car. *'Look,'* he said, *'it is beautiful, a classic Citroën DS and the price is really good too. I need to go to Paris to pick it up, but then I can take you to the hospital in comfort.* I could hardly refuse such altruism, and he needed his own transport; any potential job would be easier if he had a car. *'I am so happy,'* he told me. *'Finally, I have the car of my dreams.'* I was so pleased for him. While recovering from the operation to remove my tumour, I had time to sort all the car paperwork. Being able to speak French definitely helped.

I have never been particularly interested or impressed by any make of a car, preferring functionality over design. I can appreciate when something looks good, but do I need to sit in it and feel admired? The very thought makes me squirm in embarrassment. He was obsessed with cars, all cars, and, given the choice, his preferred vehicle would have been a Porsche or old American sports car; he was fascinated by their design and very knowledgeable, dismissing my concerns that a vintage car would come with a repair list as long as Santa's. He patiently explained to me all the reasons why it was more savvy to buy an old car. *'I have always bought vintage cars,'* he told me. *'The insurance and road tax is much lower, but people are idiots believing modern cars are much better.'*

It all made so much sense.

Chapter 25

Spring Forward

It's a good job I have such a pretty-shaped head, being bald didn't look that bad to start with, but as the rest of me fell apart or fell out, my sense of humour couldn't always save me from bouts of gloomy negativity.

One such bleak moment occurred during one of the many scans I underwent. Wheeled into this huge, dark, empty room, having been swabbed with a cool gel, I was left alone for a few minutes, and I concentrated on the machine hovering above. Fixing my gaze on that wobbly black-and-white image, I recognised the familiar shape of my non-reproductive organs and the empty space where the familiar bean shape should sit. My consultant had already explained that chemotherapy meant children were no longer an option, but in that moment, looking at that empty screen was the saddest confirmation that it would never be filled. I felt the tears slide down my face.

He agreed to accompany me to the first chemo session, and I was grateful, knowing how much he hated hospitals. I was a wreck, a bag of terrified nerves. Sitting in the high-backed chairs lining the walls, the wonderful nurses came in and attended to me, fussing and laughing and joking as they explained in detail exactly what would happen. Looking the other way as they tried to find a suitable vein (this was hard for him, being needle phobic), he immersed himself in a magazine. Waiting for them to wheel in the vats of poison for me, I translated everything they had told me so far. There was so much information, and I needed him to know and understand so he could give me the correct anti-nausea meds as soon as we left the treatment room. Nodding, he said, *'I think I might go outside for a quick roll-up. You'll be OK, won't you?'*

It could have been the fear I felt at what was about to happen, at what they were about to flood my body with, or it could have been my shock that he would suggest leaving me in the very moment I needed him most, but whatever it was, I was so angry. In a low, furious voice, I said, *'Don't you fucking dare leave me, don't you dare... how could you even think of coming back into this room smelling of smoke?'* I don't know if he thought his request was reasonable or not: *'Alright, alright,'* he said tetchily, *'I won't go.'* I sat there in the chair listening to the *beep beep* noise of the different machines carrying their dangerous liquids along channels to attack an even more dangerous enemy, and close to tears, I felt scared and let down. Was I being unreasonable? How did he not understand that it was not an appropriate thing to suggest? A few minutes passed in silence, and then he took my hand, gently caressed it, and smiled lovingly and brightly at me with no indication of the cross words exchanged a few moments before. I frowned. Had I imagined it? Had he not said it all? I looked around at the other people whose partners sat quietly next to them in supportive silence, absorbed in crosswords or drinking their tea.

This cancer must be affecting my brain, I thought.

He didn't come to any more sessions, wrinkling his nose, he told me that hospitals weren't *'his thing'*. Luckily, I had friends queueing up to take me. They sat and talked or silently held my hand, laughing with the wonderful nurses, driving me home afterwards, where he would be waiting with a fire lit in the hearth and a delicious pot of turmeric, ginger and lemon tea and some new and inspiring drawing of me on the blackboard.

The nights were the worst, the anti-nausea tablets battling with the poison inside my body, and the gut-wrenching pain and sickness keeping me awake and groaning for hours. He slept in the spare room when this was going on as it was easier. Sometimes, he heard me calling out and came into my room. Kneeling by the bed, he would fire questions at me: *'What's wrong with you? What does it feel like? What do you need?'* Impatiently demanding answers, I couldn't explain to him what was happening in English, let alone find the words in Italian. *'I can't help you if you don't tell me what it is you need me to do,'* he said, frustrated and exasperated at my inability to describe my condition in detail and furnish him with clear instructions. I was sick of being sick and of being a burden, but most of all, I was lonely.

He much preferred radiotherapy, relatively quick and clean with no *obvious* after effects, no other patients or sickness to deal with, and most importantly, no needles, so he was more than willing to attend these appointments, charming the receptionists while I was being blasted. Spring 2015 was in the air, and like the leaves on the trees outside, my hair had started to appear, my eyebrows were growing back, and the scattering of new freckles across my face made me feel as if life could happily begin again.

I felt nothing but gratitude for the amazing man who was to be my future husband. As the after-effects of the chemo started to leave my ravaged body, I remembered with love and affection how, during the worst days, he had always been there for me, taking me out for gentle walks or rushing to the local chemist to see if there was anything at all they had to alleviate the pain of going to the toilet. Coming back, he proudly relayed the story of how he had managed to explain the issue of my illness and procure the perfect remedy: a jar of prune juice. Bouncing around the kitchen like the man-sized version of Tigger, making me laugh at his antics, I realised how very lucky I was. It had been really tough on him watching me go through it all, and even worse because he had none of *his* people to talk it through, whereas my friends had constantly rallied round me. Therefore I decided he needed a surprise, something just for *him*. I found the number of some friends and organised everything. When I handed over the details of his weekend, he was utterly thrilled. *'Are you sure?'* he asked me over and over.

'You need this,' I told him. *'You need a break from all of this,'* I said, pointing at myself—my bald head and my pale face—my happiness complete at seeing how delighted he was.

Chapter 26

A Tissue

His birthday, in 2015, had been buried under a timetable of hospital appointments. Having been made aware that any special occasions had been consistently overlooked by his family, I had no intention of letting something like my cancer shelve any celebrations. Despite being at my sickest, with the help of some amazing friends, we managed to organise a treasure hunt on his birthday with a view to a special future trip for us both once I was well enough to travel. That feeling of being able to manage, organise and plan made me feel stronger as if I was turning back into the capable person I used to be.

Not the dishrag of a woman I felt when I looked in the mirror.

By the time we left for our weekend in Madrid, I had a skinhead covering of hair in a soft grey colour and pale eyebrows and eyelashes pushing their way through. I had never been any good at using scarves or wigs, but the stares and whispers from the general public were something I still found humiliating. People can often be cruel when faced with something they can't deal with. In Madrid, when he saw how upset I became, he gently told me, *'They are looking at you because you are so beautiful; you look different, but you don't look sick.'* Feeling loved and reassured, although I didn't really believe him, I adored how protective he was.

It did us the world of good being away. We ate tapas and went to see Cirque du Soleil. We laughed and felt closer to each other than we had for a long time, and for the first time in months, we decided to have sex. Actual sex. I finally felt I was ready, and I wanted to take this step back to some sort of normality despite being very nervous. My fear stemmed from a worry that nothing in my body worked quite the same anymore after everything it had been through. He was nervous, but I encouraged and reassured him, and in fact, it was OK, more than OK, even enjoyable. The relief and happiness lasted as we lay there in bed, blissed out, laughing and giggling and thankful that this part of us hadn't been destroyed.

Then I went to the toilet ... and screamed. A pain so unexpected and severe it was shocking. A burning sensation so painful it was like being knifed inside. I clenched my muscles and stopped, holding my breath; every time I tried to pee, I had to brace myself for the sheer agony.

When you go through cancer – and please ask anyone who has because I bet they will say the same – you can deal with all of the treatments, the endless medication and appointments simply because you have to. It isn't so much about being brave as accepting it as necessary. However, once the treatment is over and all the tubes removed, the one thing you never willingly come to terms with is the fear, like the sword of Damocles hanging over you, every pain, lump or bump might be a result of that bastard bit of cancer hiding somewhere the poisons couldn't find.

It was horrific in that bathroom; I was in tears, holding onto myself, barely able to breathe through the searing pain. He came running to the door, banging and shouting. *'What is it? What the hell is wrong?'* Worried sick, the two of us had the same thoughts: Had it come back? Was I part of that percentage? Luckily, we were leaving the following morning, and I booked an urgent appointment to see my doctor. There was an explanation. A direct result of all the medication had weakened things you could see, such as my hair falling out and my nails turning black, but it had a detrimental effect on the parts you couldn't see. Inside, my skin was like tissue paper;

the act of sex had shredded me in the same way a cheese grater works. *'You should have been warned,'* the doctor said regretfully as I dressed myself.

Back home, feeling relieved that there was an explanation, I translated it all in detail to my wonderful husband-to-be.

He listened carefully, far more intently than usual. Staring at me, he asked, *'So that was me? I did that to you?'*

'Yes,' I replied, *'I suppose you could put it like that.'* I didn't get his point.

Then I saw it.

He grinned, a self-satisfied smile meant only for himself, but I saw it. It was unfortunate as he immediately tried to cover it when he saw my horrified expression. He tried defending himself, but it was indefensible. *'No, no, I am just happy it is nothing serious,'* he said, trying to conceal his smirk.

And then it hit me. *'Oh my god, you think you have ripped me inside because you are so big, and you are actually proud of that.'*

He shrugged; his ego had been boosted, and he didn't need to continue the conversation.

Try as I might, I could not forget that smile.

Chapter 27

Sink Or Swim

As I grew stronger, and the toxins left my body, I found myself once again determined to find solutions to 'our' problem of his unemployment. I was capable and optimistic, and he was talented and creative, and despite life throwing the worst at us, we had tackled it all head-on.

Jobs were out there with his name on them. I was sure of it.

I found fairly lucrative house-sitting jobs for us combined with dog-sitting work, and I signed myself up to a website offering boarding for dogs and cats, as the extra cash certainly came in handy. I could easily walk and feed the charges while I was at home, and I continued to print off CVs. When he took the car for a run, he could hand them in anywhere with vacancies. Disappointingly, this proved fruitless. If the weather allowed it, he spent time on the car, lovingly cleaning and polishing every inch of it; unfortunately, this irritated me no end, and my exasperation spilled over into accusations of time that could be better used looking for work. *'You don't understand the care and attention a vintage car needs,'* he told me. *'It isn't like a modern car, it needs to be looked after; otherwise, it is simply money down the drain.'* I had it MOT'd, insured and compliant with all road rules, and if anyone queried the sense of buying a vintage car, I explained laughingly that this would, in fact, be *more economical* than a modern car. He had convinced me.

It was certainly a beautiful-looking car. Everyone said so.

Never knowingly defeated by anything, I had a seed of an idea about the car and how to turn it into a potential business opportunity and a form of employment for him. I researched wedding companies in the hope that they would add it to their books as a hire car for special occasions. Several were very interested. Printing postcards of a photo of him standing proudly in front of the car, organising public liability insurance, he quite liked the idea: *'It would be fantastic, as long as it doesn't break down,'* he said, and with that loaded sentence, a kernel of anxiety settled in my head – the idea of a bride being stuck somewhere was too terrible to contemplate. I couldn't risk it.

A friend suggested a government-funded lifeguard course, such was the desperate need in public swimming pools. Genius! Thrilled at the opportunity, I was half-tempted to enrol myself if only I had the time. He could teach kids to swim! It would be amazing, and once qualified, the money would be pretty good.

The swimming courses were a disaster.

As the teacher was (in his words) a *'bacon-eater'* who mumbled, he found it difficult to follow the classes so had no clue what was being taught. He showed little or no interest in doing any of the coursework set, the arguments inevitably followed as resentment and irritation built up into a wave of frustration and then anger. *'I don't understand any of it,'* he yelled as I sat with him and went through the exercises. Refusing point-blank to listen to explanations, he stormed off. Later, when things were calmer, he told me why it was so difficult for him: *'**You** make me shut down when I don't understand; you can't teach me as you are always angry,'* he explained. *'It scares me, I can't learn.'* Feeling awful at my inability to be a patient and kind teacher, I told him how sorry I was, and that was the end of that.

The money from the sale of the car, while a tidy amount, had not lasted forever, and we both needed to bring in a salary to pay the bills and the rent. I was anxious and it was obvious. *'That is why you were sick the last time, worrying too much about things that don't matter,'* he told me when I once again failed to laugh at some joke or comment. I must have looked incredulously at him. *'How do you think we are going to pay our rent?'* I asked.

His answer was not exactly what I was expecting: *'Just don't pay it.'*

Silence.

I must have looked confused. *'Sorry, what do you mean don't pay it?'*

It was obvious to him: *'What can they do? Kick us out? They wouldn't dare because you are still recovering.'*

Wow, quite the solution. Trying to keep calm and not shout, I asked him, *'What would we do? If they asked us to leave? What do you think? Where would we go?'*

'Live at the beach house,' he said, *'it's obvious and easy. No rent to pay, the bills are lower, life is simple: long walks on the beach, good food and less stress.'*

I could see from his expression that even he wasn't convinced by his suggestion to up sticks and move to a tiny one-bedroom place with barely enough room to unpack for a summer holiday let alone live in permanently. I listened to him talking about how much easier and simpler it would be for both of us to move over there and how much happier we could potentially be.

Would it be easier? Really?

Long walks on the beach sounded idyllic, but the reality was we'd be living in a pulled-together bedsit-style shack with no heating, no oven and no real space to sit, let alone work, too cold to hang around in during the winter and too hot in the summer, it would literally be a place to sleep. Located in a town he had frequently told me had more in common with a third-world country but with fewer work opportunities, it didn't sound like the ideal answer, no matter how I turned it around in my head.

I looked at him and considered our relationship.

I loved him and everything about him, literally everything. I believed with my whole heart that this was how relationships worked. Of course, there were ups and downs, but you fought for what you loved, working through the bad times. There was no doubt in my mind I loved him to distraction, even though I knew he had his faults. Didn't we all? Could he be an idiot? Oh yes, I wasn't totally blind to that, but he was my idiot. My goal in life was to defend, admire, love and treasure him because this was what I had signed up for. My forever. Come what may.

When the perfect job working front of house in a lovely local deli came up, I wrangled him a meeting with the manager. Even with his Italian charm and sales and merchandising experience, he managed to fail that interview. They couldn't or wouldn't say why or how he wasn't suitable for the job, but I did notice a week later that the vacancy was still being advertised. I began to have serious doubts; I was in love, but I wasn't stupid.

Chapter 28

9 TO 5

His initial love of England had started to wane.

Barbed comments about the place usually solicited an element of nodding understanding from me. I also loved the sun and the food in Italy, and it was true there was a more laid-back attitude, which went hand in hand with a far lower cost of living. In Italy, rules were something to bend or twist depending on the day of the week or the official you spoke to. There was always 'a way' to resolve a situation, whether in a post office, hospital or bank. Not so in my rigid country, the tightly adhered-to policies, rules or regulations could sometimes be viewed as unnecessary and admittedly a bit 'jobsworthy', but then again, the grass is always greener, and every country is different, but there wasn't a doubt in my mind or his that, generally speaking, in England things did actually work, despite the inclement weather.

Another depressing factor was our social life, which had become almost obsolete. He was no longer interested in what he defined as the '*English way*' of having a good time, usually involving copious quantities of alcohol or dinner at friends' houses. He also disliked pubs, finding them cold, expensive, and a waste of time, sitting around people with whom he had little in common and nothing to say to them. We stayed at home more and more, adding to his overall dissatisfaction.

He began viciously criticising everyone and their lifestyle: *'People here never do anything,'* he grumbled. *'You never see anyone.'* He indicated the empty streets when we were out driving or walking around. *'All English people do is stay inside their houses, hiding from everyone, drinking until they are drunk, then after the weekend, they go to work, head down, miserable, and work work work until they can drink again.'*

Feeling heavy with the weight of his sweeping judgements, exhausted justifying people I didn't know in order to make the one I thought I did know feel better, I often ended up agreeing with him to facilitate a lighter atmosphere. However, his unpleasant thoughts on total strangers weren't sitting comfortably anymore; if anything, it had become boring. Nor did I support his theories about the *'bacon-eaters'*, and I couldn't be coerced into a unanimous panning or laugh along at his biting observations. Offended, he said, *'You don't laugh anymore like you used to, you are not fun.'* I tried to say that the name-calling and constant slating of everything English was hard to take. Immediately backtracking, he said, *'I'm only joking.'* Looking hurt, he asked me, *'Why do you have to take everything so seriously now?'*

At a loss as to what to say or do anymore, defeated by the sheer dullness of his endless bitching about everything and everyone, I asked him, *'If you hate it so much here, why do you stay?'* I wasn't asking him to leave, but I really wanted to know. *'If everything about our lives is so awful, why don't you go back to Italy?'*

His response was fast and nasty.

'Is that what you want? For me to go back? So you can carry on your life without me?' He was furious. How dare I offer options, choices he himself could make. He was angry and shouted, *'Of course, you want me to go back, after I have given up EVERYTHING to be here with you.'* Ignoring him and refusing to rise to his endless baiting, he followed me triumphantly around the flat. *'That's it, isn't it? You want to be on your own in your office glued to your laptop and on the phone to your friends because you are incapable of a relationship.'*

This continued until I was so confused that I completely forgot what the original discussion was about.

Leaving *him* was never an option.

With me on the road to recovery and back working full time again, with the summer holidays far behind us and winter looming, I had had enough. I loved him very much, but this wouldn't work if he didn't. No longer interested in an extended pointless argument with me nagging and shouting my frustrations, I was simply over his excuses for not finding some sort of employment.

In a soft voice, I calmly told him: '*Either you find a job, or we are over, it is entirely up to you*'.

My words briefly stopped him in his tracks, but not the manner in which they were spoken. Throwing his arms up in the air to express his exasperation, he ranted, '*Oh, here we go again. All my fault as usual, just because* they *didn't give me the job in that stupid shop.*' Watching me closely, waiting for my retaliation and raised voice, he was surprised to see me shrug my shoulders and smile sadly at him; there was nothing left to say.

He stormed out, and I heard him slam the car door and accelerate away. Breathing deeply, I felt both relief he had gone and concern that I may have been too harsh. Hours later, he returned with a massive smile on his face. Dancing around, he waved a piece of paper, laughing delightedly. Having driven into town, he had found a vacancy at a large high-street clothing shop, had an interview and was immediately hired as a sales assistant. It was all I had ever wanted, for him and for me. I fulfilled my side of the bargain, becoming the personification of the perfect adoring girlfriend, for the few months he worked there. I was the taxi, the cook and the maid, making sure he knew how wonderful and appreciated he was. He took a well-earned break after Christmas; he was shattered and his legs ached.

It turned out the break was a permanent one as the company ended his contract. Masking his delight at having been absolved of all responsibility for his newly established unemployment status, he was once again as free as a bird. I was more than a little mystified at how, after three months of working in an environment where he had contact with the same people every almost every day, he had not made a single friend.

Chapter 29

Could Do Better/B+

Back when I was at university, my friend and I went to see a tarot card reader; for a laugh, we told each other.

That wasn't strictly true. I went because I wanted confirmation (from a higher source) that I would leave university with a degree. Despite attending most of the lectures, I couldn't be classed as a model student, so I reckoned a fiver invested in Mystic Margaret was worth the sound advice she might offer, enabling me to complete the year and my dissertation with optimism and faith. I can't remember if she verified my hoped-for result, but I clearly remember her firm belief that my studying would not necessarily finish with a degree.

There was more book learning to come.

I had spent three years scraping through that degree. I loved French because I had an ear for languages, but economics felt like pulling teeth on a daily basis as I was not a natural academic. My dissertation was based on The Common Agricultural Policy (I'm not even kidding), which my poor Dad agreed to check for typos and had the two of us climbing the walls in frustration; his comment '*It has some interesting points*' made me realise just how diplomatic that man was.

Nearly thirty years later, and with plenty of hindsight, I can see that what 'Margaret' told me was less an ability to predict the future and more of a generic fact. We never really stop studying, learning, training, improving, and pretty much anything we can do to upgrade our lives: a better car, house, wardrobe, whatever it is. As human beings, many of us have something inside that spurs us on to have, do, and be better. Not everyone carries on formal studying, but starting any new job, whether physical or mental, brings with it that first week of overwhelming fatigue as our brains absorb reams of new information, and our bodies take us to bed early enough to rest and regenerate so that we can cope with the next new day. Like our school-days, except then we had the added stress of physically growing.

Every day, we absorb new information and go back home to sleep so our bodies and brains expand and develop, ready to start another day of knowledge: a hamster wheel of non-stop production as we work to improve upon everything we have learnt. It's a knackering process which sometimes works beautifully depending on where your strengths and weaknesses lie, creative or academic, from primary through to secondary school, we are graded, tested, judged and scored on everything we have done in that one environment, all condensed in a flowery or damning piece of paper given to the parents twice a year: the dreaded school report.

Mine boiled down to pretty much the same sentence written in different ways:

Good student but room for improvement / Good effort but must try harder / Good work but for better results needs to apply herself / If she concentrated more and was less distracted could be excellent/ Shows aptitude but needs improvement.

I showed signs of great capability, but I always fell slightly short of my full potential. At the start of every school year, every term, I was determined it was going to be different – *I* was going to be different. My exercise books would be neater, my homework would be completed not just on time but early, making me the teacher's favourite. I would remember everything, and my pencil case would remain immaculate for the entire term.

It was never going to happen.

In the same way, those enviable kids in my class, renowned for their spectacularly neat handwriting or beautifully kept books, would never doodle on their exercise books, bring in the wrong pencils or lose their essays. It was the way of the world. We rarely change our identities as written up by those acutely observing us on a daily basis; if we do, it is only short-term, like a sudden growth spurt.

I once changed schools mid-term, and in the new one, they told me I didn't have to take the chemistry exam as it was a relatively new subject for me. Being the belligerent, stubborn arse I am, I swallowed the periodic table night after night, coming up with ways of remembering those chemical formulas, learning them backwards, forwards and sideways. I aced that exam just to prove a point. The school thought they had signed up the next new junior prize-winning science genius. Having proved I was capable, I reverted to my usual stance of '*Could do better*', much to the chagrin of my poor mother.

Those three words became a mild indoctrination, as if all those years of reading about how much better I could and would be if I just tried harder were stamped somewhere in my hippocampus, the part of my brain where ingrained memories have had a lasting impact on my everyday behaviour. Is that what our school reports have done in some way? Influenced our behaviour in day-to-day situations, made us cling on with tenacity to make a situation better? If you aced your exams and were an A* student throughout, do you have the best marriage or career or house? Is everything filed neatly away where you can find it at a moment's notice, and do you always know what to do and how to do it? I believe there is room for improvement within us all, and I am not blaming my schooldays for being a bit disorganised. Ultimately, what makes the world go round are those very differences and abilities. Then again, according to my cod psychology above, could it be rooted in my childhood belief that I always could do better?

I was in a relationship where my fingertips (in the very wise words of Kate Nash's deliciously eloquent song) appeared to be holding onto the cracks in our foundation. It was weak to give up, walk away, not try *everything*. My first marriage had painfully demonstrated how easy it had been for him to walk away, and I carried that ingrained feeling of failure personally. One minute, it had been good, and then suddenly, it wasn't, giving me no choice, no discussion and no chance to improve it.

That was not going to happen again.

I had no doubt that if I aimed a little higher, I could definitely do better and turn this relationship into the gold shiny star status it warranted.

Chapter 30

Moving On

When he called me from Italy, I could hear the breathless excitement in his voice. *'Just hear me out,'* he pleaded before I had even opened my mouth. *'This place is unbelieveable, I never even knew it was here, you can't imagine the peace, the weather, the views, we could definitely live here.'*

From my office in our flat in the West Sussex green belt, with a beautiful view of the countryside, I listened to his animated voice as he called me from outside the hospital where he had taken his dad for a routine operation. He was describing a small, beautiful Umbrian town situated on a lake, only forty-five minutes from his parents' house. He had already made enquiries about renting there, the cost of which, apparently, was less than half of what we were paying in the UK.

The fact that he was excited it was close to his parents was interesting as he'd never expressed more than the bare minimum interest in what any of them were up to; if anything, it had been dreadful stories of his childhood and his controlling mother, the sister who cared about nothing but work and buying (according to him) endless rubbish to fill her empty life. Suddenly, living closer to them had become a key factor. He was tugging at a sensitive part of me as I had spent so much time with my own dad over the last few years. How could I refuse?

Sensing a weakening in my resolve to remain in England, he played his ace card: '*You, in particular, need to live somewhere where you can be totally stress-free,*' he said. '*It will be so good for your health, so good for you to stop and just enjoy life. We cannot risk you being unwell again.*'

Quite the mic drop moment. My Prince Charming only wanted the very best for me.

It was 2016, and we were planning our wedding for later that year in Italy. Something about his words resonated, and his healthcare warning seemed appropriate and timely. After everything he had been through, it felt like the right time to live in *his* country. He had spent almost four years doing everything possible to try and work in England, and then there had been the devastating effect of my illness. We were out and on the other side of that, so perhaps it was time for a seismic change. I just wanted us to be happy, and if that meant being back in Italy, then OK – a relationship is all about compromise.

I had one caveat, though. He had to find work; otherwise, I was not moving.

The single-minded determination he demonstrated upon his return was impressive. He spent hours searching job sites and sending his CV to everyone he could think of. He turned into a proactive, focused and dynamic individual, and I was relieved. This wasn't the time for recriminations regarding his previous lackadaisical attitude. I was proud and astonished when he was offered his dream job as a visual merchandiser. Furthermore, after training, he would be required to work in a location a very convenient twenty-minute drive from the very town he had decided would be ideal for us to live in. It was as if we had been sent this undeniable proof (the universe or gods or stars or whatever had all aligned) that after several difficult years, things were going to work out for us.

I could barely contain my delight at his success on the job front, the move to Italy, and all the implications: a wedding to plan and a beautiful new part of the country to explore together. There was something else to be over the moon about too. My dream had always been to write, and although I had penned a few magazine articles and blogs, I had been too busy to spend any real time on it. Now, there was a real chance I could stop working and focus on writing. The idea of exploring that further, no longer worrying about money and being 'looked after' while he worked, was everything I had ever hoped for.

On telling him how delighted I was at this turn of events, my eyes shone with love and gratitude, and he looked at me happily. *'My fattt dirrrtttyyy girlfriend,'* he laughingly said, using the comical nickname he had lovingly bestowed upon me and used instead of my actual name. *'Yes, finally, you can write as much as you like, and if you want to teach a little bit, you can also do that for extra money.'* He added this as if teaching was an easy sideline hustle I did with my eyes closed. I didn't say anything, but the truth was I didn't want to teach anymore.

Telling my wonderful dad was the downside, and I felt torn. Even though I wasn't going until I had completed the school year and would be around until the summer, it was still a difficult conversation, for me at least. As usual, he handled it perfectly. I was to do what was right for me, always. *'You have to do whatever you think is right, and don't live your life for anyone else,'* he told me. *'Of course, I will miss you, but visits back and forth will be easy enough,'* he reassured me. With his blessing, I felt as if I could have lived on the moon, as long as I knew my dad approved.

* * *

The job he had found required him to complete training first, so he was gone long before the packing boxes arrived. I had a full-time job and the entire apartment to pack up, not to mention finding international movers who would also take his car over to Italy at a reasonable price. Kissing me goodbye, impatient to start this exciting new phase of his life, he repeated the instructions for the twentieth time: *'I will see you soon. Please make sure the removal company know how to pack my car properly.'* I would have plenty to keep me busy over the coming months.

My feelings of sadness or mild regret at leaving my home, my friends and my dad, and even the lovely school where I worked were quashed by those close to me excitedly talking about my new life in Italy, reminding me constantly how lucky I was. It certainly seemed idyllic, moving to a stunning lakeside town on the border between Umbria and Tuscany with a gorgeous husband-to-be waiting for me AND a glamorous wedding planned in Rome. There wasn't time to feel anything but blissed-out happiness about my life and where it was headed, so I pushed any doubts I had to the back of my mind, concentrating instead on the sparkling future ahead.

He called me infrequently with hurried calls telling me how difficult it all was: '*I am working all day and then I have to sort out viewings on different places, it is almost impossible,*' he explained wearily. '*I am so tired. I barely have time to eat.*' I asked about his work, eager to know how he was settling into his dream job: '*How is it all going? Do you like the people? Is the work interesting?*' His answers were brief: '*Good, I like it, the people are nice, but we have a new manager starting next week.*' He didn't elaborate, so I changed tack and tried asking about the properties he had seen. Again, there was little he was able to tell me except how hard it was to find the right one. I hadn't been over to see the town yet, placing my entire trust in his knowledge of the area and the sort of place we would need, reassuring him that we could and would make any property our own as we had always done. Trying to help out, I had sent links to potential rental properties online, suggesting their suitability, but he was having none of it: '*No, they are no good,*' he said. '*You don't understand, it has to be in the right place.*' He was right. I was having less and less of a clue about anything over there. Evidently, the pressure of holding down a job and finding a suitable apartment in his own country with his family on standby weighed heavily on his beautiful, tanned, freckled shoulders.

Home alone and surrounded by a sea of cardboard, I found that each time I finished one room, another sprang up demanding to be sorted, folded or sold. I started out very much in the spirit of those brand-new exercise books they handed out at the beginning of a new term: perfectly taped, labelled, and stored methodically. That initial diligent efficiency very quickly evaporated as clothes, objects and books appeared to be haemorrhaging from storage spaces I had hitherto been unaware of. Becoming less meticulous and more ruthless, I binned items deemed as unnecessary and anything of any value I sold to the highest bidder, friends or the local school fair. I no longer cared about the weight of the boxes or how they were labelled, I just needed them filled up and gone.

As so often happens, life has this habit of coming together with a timetabled precision, making us laugh about the absurdity of stressing over nothing. He found an apartment, a perfect one, with views over the lake, managing to negotiate a decent rent. He excitedly told me everything: *'I can't wait for you to see the place. It is so wonderful and in exactly the right location.'* Now I had an address, I was able to book the movers, and we had a date for them to take everything I had packed to our new life in Italy.

And breathe...

Life was exciting. We were getting married, and I was moving —the proverbial fairytale ending. It was beyond anything I could have dreamed, and things would be just fine. That belief kept me going, holding onto it the same way a drowning man holds onto a small piece of polystyrene believing it will save him, keep him afloat.

Sure, it might work for a while...

Chapter 31

Home Sweet Home

I went to Italy to see him and the apartment in the town where our immediate future would lie.

His excitement was palpable as he and his father picked me up from the small airport, and we set off to see our 'home'. As we drove along the main road, they both watched my expression carefully, anticipating my reaction. Their enthusiasm was contagious, and as a beautiful lake came into sight on the left-hand side, I made all the right noises. It wasn't difficult, as the lake shimmered in the sunlight, and in front of me, my boyfriend clapped his hands enthusiastically. *'I cannot believe this was just down the road from my parents' house all this time,'* he exclaimed. *'All this time and I never knew it existed,'* he mused. I nodded, taking in the surroundings. It did seem strange, considering it was so close, but swept along in the moment, I didn't say anything about it.

The apartment he had found for us was in a building on the main road surrounding the borgo, right next to the historical town walls. *'Don't look at the building, it isn't very attractive,'* he said, with a hint of disappointment. It was a boxy post-war palazzo, and I knew how much he preferred the older style villas to this, but I was genuinely impressed, and he had been right, location was fundamental. Nothing prepared me for the stunning views as we opened the door to our place, and giddy with excitement, he told me to close my eyes until we were through the door.

Much bigger than I had imagined and flooded with light from the tall windows, I was suitably speechless, but the glittering prize was, without a doubt, the breathtaking view of the massive lake from nearly every window. He looked expectantly at me. '*Wow*,' I said in awe, '*this is amazing.*' Satisfied at my impressed gasps and exclamations of pleasure at his efforts, he smiled at me, and we all trooped out for a celebratory lunch.

During that swift visit, he introduced me to locals and neighbours he had met and apparently made friends with. Everyone seemed warm, welcoming, and curious about our reasons for moving there. It was certainly a very pretty place with bars and restaurants, gift shops and small local businesses. Below the historical part of town, there were more facilities all around the lake, which stretched on for miles: cycle paths and parks as well as small lakeside beaches. I could definitely see myself living here. I couldn't wait to start.

I had seen it, touched it and even tasted how good it was going to be, but for now, I had to put everything in order back in England. As far as I was concerned, there was no fresh start if you left a mess behind.

I had emptied our apartment, cleaned it and handed back the keys. Now, the plan was to finish the school term while staying at my dad's house before heading off in the summer to finalise wedding plans and settle into our new home. In the meantime, I had taken on a few days of dog-walking and house-sitting, and it was at one such house he called me one evening.

I could immediately hear in his voice that something wasn't right. It was about his job: the new manager was creating a vile work environment. Holding my breath as the all too familiar lament started up, I listened. '*She won't let me do any of the visual merchandising, she sends me down to the warehouse and refuses to let me touch any of the displays.*' His voice was trembling, he sounded close to tears. I was more than a little puzzled at this turn of events. *'I thought you had been trained specifically for that role?'* I said in a kind tone so he didn't think I was having a go at him.

'Yes, I was, but she has made it clear she is not interested in my input.' After a pause, he added *'Everyone hates her,'* underlining this was a general feeling and in no way had anything to do with him personally. Inwardly sighing and guessing at the next part, he surprised me when he declared stubbornly, *'I am not leaving, I need this job.'* I exhaled, relief washing over me, agreeing a good idea would be to contact the training manager with whom he had been friendly. Perhaps he could define the role? Ask him for something in writing so there are no misunderstandings.

Tiny alarm bells were ringing somewhere, but I silenced them. I had my own worries as my dad had some health issues—his heart, his big, beautiful heart.

Chapter 32

Unconditional

Time at my dad's can be summed up in three words: comfortable, peaceful and safe. It felt like a treat.

I didn't have to worry about him, or whether he was being 'entertained', as ever since he had found himself alone, he had developed his own schedule of regular habits. Every Saturday, he ate his favourite cheeses and crackers as a light lunch; he was pretty good about his diet and his health, making sure he ate a decent range of fruit and vegetables, but he also knew when and how often to indulge. Sports viewing schedules were set up on the TV or on his computer, depending on which channels were broadcasting the games. These were timetabled into his routine and accompanied by a mug of tea or a can of his favourite beer, depending on the time of day.

He kept his garden beautifully and, despite lamenting the amount of clutter in the house and things on his to-do list, he systematically worked his way through. Having read articles about keeping dementia at bay by stretching your brain use, he was diligent about making time to read the paper, religiously complete the crossword and work his way through the sudoku puzzle book. Sometimes, I'd find him standing in front of the kitchen window quietly watching the birds gather around the various feeders, filled to the brim with seeds, while, at the same time, keeping an eye out for any *'damned squirrels'*. Plotting his revenge against those thieving vermin was another small joy for him, and he devised various ingenious traps to keep the bird food safe from the *'bushy-tailed tossers'*.

Pulling into the driveway, any tension I had melted out of me and my shoulders relaxed. Walking up to the front door and following our hello hug, Dad would smile his *'Cup of tea?'* offer and lead me into the kitchen to stick the kettle on. Reassuring routines I instantly relaxed into. He loved company, home-cooked food and someone to share a bottle of his best wine with, and I was more than happy to oblige.

An exchange so perfect I'm not sure who benefitted from it more.

Spending time with him meant no pressure to be anything other than *myself*. Sometimes, we went to the pub or chose fish and chips as a cheeky dinner, and he always paid. Offering money for my part was met with a bemused expression. I was his daughter, and as far as he was concerned, it simply wasn't the done thing.

It wasn't one-sided. My part of the bargain included spending time in the kitchen cooking his favourite meals to fill up his freezer. Shopping in the local Sainsbury's for the ingredients while he waited in the car outside listening to BBC Radio 4 launched me into his good books as he loathed grocery shopping, *'Are you sure you don't need me to come in with you?'* he would ask, his eyes sparkling in delight at the prospect of sitting in his warm, comfortable car listening to the news while he waited. Grinning at him and grabbing the pile of meticulously folded plastic shopping bags, I would head inside. Trying to convince him that this was like a day out for me would have been too difficult; I love grocery shopping in Sainsbury's the way some people love handbags.

Listening to my music and cooking all the different dishes in his kitchen, I was in my element, my dad regularly popping in from the garden or the garage or when a rugby game permitted the half-time break. Smiling at me, he would say with characteristic understatement, *'Some-*

thing smells good', and I'd hand him a spoon to sample whatever I was cooking so I could adjust it accordingly; after all, he would be eating it: the chicken and mushroom casserole I had worked so hard on to make as much like Mum's as possible, (*a bit more cream, maybe*) the chicken curry (*a touch more chillies, please*) or the Thai fishcakes (*perfect!*). Then, once cool enough, he would label them in their Tupperware boxes, all evenly portioned out by me, and with a satisfied smile, pack them into perfectly arranged freezer drawers.

His happiness made mine.

He was lovely, stubborn, and both endlessly patient and impatient, depending on who he was dealing with; we regularly exchanged stories of grumpy frustration with local councils, politicians, bad drivers and crappy pub food. Watching TV together, we had our favourites: nature programmes, *Line of Duty* and *University Challenge*; I concentrated hard on the latter because answering a question correctly earned his beaming smile of impressed approval, turning me into an eleven-year-old with a particularly good school report.

Sometimes, I would make his favourite roast lamb with all the trimmings he loved and bring it in on a tray so he could carry on watching whatever important match was on; a few minutes later, sticking my head around the door to check he didn't need anything else, his delighted expression telling me I had hit a home run.

I stayed with my dad longer than expected that summer with good reason; he needed an operation to have a stent put in around his heart. I have never met anyone who wanted to be less of a nuisance than my dad, the personification of patience and kindness until it came to travel insurance companies or the music of Frank Sinatra – even he had his limits. That patience multiplied a hundred times when dealing with the NHS. Because he had so much respect and admiration for them, he refused point-blank to 'hassle' them for an earlier operation date. *'They know I'm waiting, they will call when a space becomes available,'* he told me when I complained once again about the lack of an update. I wanted him by my side at my wedding, and the weeks were fast closing in. He needed the procedure and time to recover, but time was passing, and we still had no date. With his agreement, I took over on his behalf and made countless calls to doctors and hospital administration staff pleading my case. They eventually relented; everyone wants a happy ending; and the additional story of this romantic wedding in Rome definitely helped. He was in.

My dad was going to be there with me on my special day.

I adored spending time with him as much as I missed spending time with my husband-to-be. 'Torn' is not a word to be used lightly, but I felt ripped apart every time I said goodbye to one adored male figure to be with the other equally missed and loved one.

Only one made me feel safe, though.

Chapter 33

Family Ties

By the time I arrived in Italy to live there full-time, he was no longer employed.

His time (he told me) was spent making as many connections as possible within the new town we were living in. Apparently, it was the only way to find work in Italy; it was all about the schmoozing. I couldn't possibly understand as I was English and things were done differently, but finally, he was in charge of making it happen, and it would be OK. I believed him: *his* country, *his* language and *his* people.

Was I happy about it? Well, yes, because in many respects, I was living the dream: an imminent magical wedding to plan for, the summer to look forward to with endless sunshine and time to familiarise ourselves with our new home on the Umbrian/Tuscan border, with his family just down the road. The little town had plenty of bars and restaurants, providing numerous job opportunities; he was spoilt for choice. Finding work before had been no problem for him, and if necessary, I could always look for something to tide us over; it was all peachy.

Wasn't it?

In the meantime, our new place kept us busy, not least because it was two-thirds smaller than our flat in the UK, and we had to find space for all our stuff. When I mentioned the number of still unpacked boxes when I arrived, he instantly reminded me of the difficulties he had overcome in negotiating contracts and being available when it all turned up. During these discussions, I felt myself straightening up and looking at him, saying, '*I did a lot too, you know,*' or maybe I just thought it, scared of actually saying aloud how tough I had found it, leaving my dad, packing up four years of our lives and ending a secure job, mainly because I knew it would be met with a rolling of the eyes and comments like '*Why is everything a competition to you? Does it matter who did what?*' and his killer line: '*Why do you always turn everything good and positive into something else?*'

Afraid of my draining negativity and not wanting to be that person, I said nothing, shutting out that niggle of resentment, ignoring it because life was too good and too short to waste on petty arguments about one-upmanship.

> **COGNITIVE DISSONANCE**
> SOMETHING NOT NECESSARILY WRONG BUT ALSO SOMETHING NOT QUITE RIGHT; YOU DON'T WANT TO ADMIT TO IT BECAUSE IT DOESN'T MAKE LOGICAL SENSE. IT DOESN'T FEEL RIGHT, BUT LOOKING FROM THE OUTSIDE IN, THERE SEEMS NOTHING TO WORRY ABOUT. A FORM OF DENIAL AND AN UNDENIABLE PART OF BEING BROKEN DOWN, DOUBTING WHAT YOU WOULD NORMALLY UNDERSTAND OR AT LEAST RECOGNISE. REMEMBER WHEN HESTON BLUMENTHAL MADE FOOD THAT LOOKED LIKE ONE THING BUT TASTED LIKE SOMETHING ENTIRELY DIFFERENT? SAVOURY ICE LOLLIES OR BACON-AND-EGG ICE CREAM. THAT'S THE DELICIOUS VERSION; IT ISN'T SO GREAT WHEN IT IS YOURSELF THAT YOU NO LONGER RECOGNISE OR TRUST. A SUBTLE FORM OF BRAINWASHING, AND IT IS CLEVER, VERY, VERY CLEVER BECAUSE IT IS OFTEN HIDDEN IN FOLDS OF APPARENT KINDNESS.

As we settled in that summer of 2016, his dad would regularly drive the 50 km to see us, almost a two-hour round trip, but his delight at spending time with his son was obvious. He was in his late seventies but incredibly dynamic and looked decades younger. I really enjoyed his company and didn't mind listening to the same story for the hundredth time because he wanted to feel important; I thought it was a small price to pay to finally belong to this family and feel I was part of something *conventional*. I knew they had previously had problems, but I naively believed in a reconciliation now that we all lived pretty close together.

My idea of an Italian version of *The Waltons* seriously missed the mark.

His dad would regularly turn up without warning, and it could be anytime from early morning to lunchtime. He was bored since retiring and craved company. But his 'surprise' visits before 8 a.m. caused my future husband to whinge endlessly about his father's selfishness and lack of consideration. As I calmed him down, telling him it was only for a few hours, his attitude would change, viewing the visit as an opportunity and encouraging me to regale his dad of all the things we needed money for, perhaps even persuading him to buy the apartment as an investment. *'Just talk to him about it as an option, please,'* he begged me. The idea of asking someone I barely knew for money appalled me. *'He listens to you, he respects you, just mention how much we need, plant the seed,'* he said, almost physically pushing me forward towards the door as his dad approached. It was unpleasant and awkward, and I refused, feeling bad because I wanted to please him. But hinting to his father that we needed money was humiliating and a line I was not prepared to cross. Backing off, I could sense his irritation, but seeing how uneasy it made me feel, he eventually stopped asking.

We often went out for lunch with his dad to the local restaurants, which initially was lovely and an opportunity to catch up. But it turned into two to three times a week, and I just couldn't manage eating regular three-course meals with copious amounts of alcohol in the middle of the day, especially not with a wedding dress to fit into. He, on the other hand, ordered food as if it was his last meal on earth: first, second and third courses, usually opting for a fillet steak with side orders of vegetables, fries, and salad, followed by dessert. We never ate that much at home, not even on the rare occasions we went out. Ordering just one dish and refusing more, he pressed me to choose something else: *'Don't worry,'* he told me, *'he's paying because he wants to.'* Alcohol at these lunches was consumed as if it was going out of fashion: pre-lunch drinks, wine during the meal and coffee with some sort of spirit or digestif at the end. Now, I am no teetotaller, an occasional glass of wine at lunch, and I will happily indulge, but excessive daytime drinking literally wipes me out. I could abstain with no problem, but my main objection and concern was for his dad, who had to drive home half-cut, drunk, wobbly on his feet, semi-paralytic; call it what you like, but it wasn't safe. I would insist we go for another coffee or for a walk to sober him up, waste time, anything but have him drive the distance back home. *'He'll be fine,'* he said, waving his dad off as he weaved his way down the road.

My worries about his dad's alcohol consumption and driving were generally ridiculed, and my suggestions of maybe limiting it to one bottle of wine or no spirits after lunch were shot down. I was a cultural killjoy and didn't understand the *'Italian way'*. My very English preoccupation with drink driving was considered a general joke. With a captive audience of the restaurant staff, he laughingly explained how we had to *stay overnight* with friends in England if we were drinking. *'It doesn't work like that here,'* he said, smiling and stroking my cheek in amusement as they poured more wine, looking at me with pity and curiosity.

I stopped going for lunch.

It was only natural he was spoiled by his father, and pointing out how lucky I was, he told me, *'You have a great relationship with your dad, I have never had that,'* making me feel terribly sorry for him, so if his father bought him lunch or gave him money for petrol or car repairs, I felt it was sweet as he was trying to make up to him.

Chapter 34

Wedding Bells

My first wedding was an incredibly traditional affair in a church in a very English town with a 1950s American car, me in a big white dress with feathers, a cake and a sit-down meal.

My second wedding could not have been more different. Everyone who attended said it was the most beautiful, cool, and stylish affair. The amazing ceremony, held a stone's throw from the Colosseum and bang in the middle of incredible history, was packed with some of the most gorgeous people from all over the world celebrating our day. A photographic shoot on Vespas with our friends, zooming around the city with unscheduled stops at beautiful landmarks to take laughing, natural shots. We veered in and out of the traffic to the sounds of cars beeping and honking their horns at our unbelievable happiness. Lunch followed in a central trattoria with typical Roman dishes such as *fiori di zucca* (deep-fried courgette flowers with mozzarella and anchovies), *spaghetti alla carbonara, bucatini alla matriciana* and *saltimbocca* followed by tiramisu. You name it, we had thought of it to make this the best experience possible. Bi-lingual speeches in the restaurant and, in the evening, a huge party in stunning gardens and an actual Roman grotto situated on the most ancient road of all, The Appian Way.

However, it didn't start off perfectly.

I had no idea that, during the summer when my Dad was having his heart stent sorted in hospital, he also had a scan to check a small bleed, discovering quite by accident something far more serious: lung cancer. Swearing his doctors to secrecy, he hid that from me when I went to pick him up, hiding it from everyone so that our big day wasn't ruined. On the actual day, he took a wrong turn trying to find the taxi we had sent to pick him up and lost his way to the ceremony. I am struggling to write this without crying, as the idea of him being alone and worried still upsets me.

Waiting in the car outside the venue, they called me: '*He isn't here, we don't know where he is.*' My heart was racing and I was close to tears, refusing to go ahead until he was found. A mad panic ensued as the registry office staff were assured he was on his way while various members of the family and friends looked for him. I had no intention of going anywhere until my dad arrived safe and sound.

My future husband walked over to the car and opened the door. As I climbed out, dozens of my friends were watching and taking photographs of me in my satin dove grey 1950s dress and ballet pumps. Seeing them all, I smiled while asking him through my worried tears, '*Is he here?*' Seeing the state I was in over my missing dad, he reassured me, '*It will be fine, don't worry about your dad, he'll turn up... but guess what happened to me? You can't imagine what I have been through this morning. A total nightmare! I've had so many problems, but I sorted everything.*'

Looking up through the crowd of friends, I suddenly saw him, breathless, red-faced, apologising to anyone and everyone for causing a delay. He had somehow found his way in this foreign city, managing to explain to someone in a bar that he needed a taxi urgently, remembering, too, the name of the location of his daughter's wedding. *My dad*, who had paid for the whole thing because *my husband-to-be's* family had never offered to pay a single euro towards the day, much less turn up. *My dad*, who was my whole world, had been lost in Rome yet had managed to find a place he had never been to with a secret tumour in his lung and a newly installed heart stent. *My dad* who had never inconvenienced a single person in his life.

As my dad walked me into that opulent room with all those beautiful and glamorous guests, the people I loved most in the world, beaming their encouragement while I tightly held his arm and squeezed away his unnecessary apologies, and there, standing before me, I saw the '*man*' I had decided was a good idea to invest my entire future in.

Did I have any doubts about what I was about to do? Yes, I did, but I pushed them down, way down, covering them up in the thoughts of what was to come, the people surrounding me, the beautiful red cocktail dress I would be wearing later, the stunning party that night on the Appian Way. I thought, too, of the years together and not together and everything we had overcome.

We were to be married. Isn't that what I had always wanted? This good-looking, gorgeous, caring man in front of me with his slick suit and fancy handmade shoes with no visible socks and his light-hearted way of joking with all his friends in this beautiful, serious setting. *The Happy Ending*. It certainly felt that way when I left the registry office and stepped onto the beautiful piazza with so many of our friends and my family cheering and congratulating us.

I had organised a surprise for him with all my friends and family. A standard joke of his was the English and Germans' dreadful habit of wearing socks with sandals. In the months leading up to the wedding, I had invited everyone to bring sandals or flip-flops and socks to wear in a photo as a joke, a sweet, thoughtful and funny thing to make my new husband laugh, a funny memory to look back on. Everyone I knew participated in this gesture of self-deprecation and ironic humour. Not a single Italian had felt inclined to join in the joke despite being invited to participate, watching in amusement while the photos were taken. Immediately afterwards, his friends requested their own photo: '*All the old crowd,*' they yelled to each other, and everyone he had known all his life gathered for a smiling, hugging, happy photo around the grinning groom.

I was not asked to be in the photo.

Surrounded by the friends and family I loved, I enjoyed every part of that long day, having wonderful catch-ups with them all, leaving no time to wonder where he disappeared to for several hours in the afternoon. Later, joining the main evening party together, he bathed in the success of it all, introducing me to people he had often talked about but spending no time whatsoever with the dozens of guests who had travelled hundreds and even thousands of miles for our special day; a quick hello and a handshake and he was off again, the bronzed sockless social butterfly, glass of wine in hand, laughing, joking and smoking with people he had known his whole life.

When our surprise wedding cake was brought out and surrounded by sparklers and people vying to take photographs, I jokingly smeared a bit of cream on his face for fun... a silly, playful moment. Big mistake. He immediately tensed, although only I could see his jaw tightening. Under his breath, still smiling to cover his irritation, he asked me, *'Why would you do that?'* wiping it from his jawline, careful not to dirty his shirt collar or let anyone see his expression. My face fell as I felt ashamed and stupid, but before I could think about it for one second longer, he took me in his arms and kissed me in a perfect photo opportunity.

Everyone around us cheered, conveniently drowning out the distant sound of those alarm bells going off.

Chapter 35

Chinese Whispers

There is nothing quite like a wedding and a honeymoon to distract you from reality. However, soon after returning to the apartment, there was no time to settle down to married life because I had work to do.

The summer before the wedding, I had enjoyed working for a week in a high-end designer sample sale; it was fun and reaped benefits as buying several items of expensive clothing at sample sale prices then selling them online had proved lucrative. Then, I was offered a job for a month as a runner in the same Italian fashion house showroom in Milan. It was too much money to turn down. The person offering me the job was a friend of a friend, and after agreeing it would be good opportunity, he arranged for me to stay with some friends in the city while he remained in the little Umbrian village to 'network' with the locals.

I didn't like Milan but I truly hated that job: one long month of visiting international buyers being shown the latest collection. I found myself running up and down a shop floor the length of a football pitch, looking for the correct products for the sales team to show off, with every bag, belt and clothing line having a name or a code I could never remember and could care even less about, I counted down the days till I was out of there. Each morning, I dragged myself to work, dreading the forthcoming superficiality, and every evening, I walked back feeling slightly lighter knowing I was closer to the finish line. Despite my aching feet and legs and the 'lollipop look' (a big head perched on my tall, skinny body) I had developed from lack of proper food, I happily knew that there was a definite reward coming, the distant icing on the cake (that no one ever ate): my new husband was only days away from picking me up. Day in, day out, pretending I wasn't physically and mentally exhausted by pandering to a bunch of badly dressed rich people, frustrated and proud of my inability (refusal) to care enough to learn the names of handbag ranges, which individually, were the price of a terraced house.

Towards the end of the contract, I was passing the very friend who had recommended the job, and we exchanged pleasantries and future plans now the end was in sight. Smiling teasingly, I said to her, *'It's all your fault I'm here,'* and she laughed, replying she hoped it hadn't been that bad, and we went on with the day, both in good spirits as the end was in sight, a huge relief for *everyone*.

My metaphorical shining knight would soon be rescuing me from this ridiculously pretentious world, and I would be over the moon to see him, which I was... initially. Arriving at the showroom, charming all the normally extremely surly receptionists, he swung me round and round in front of them all, saying, *'My wife, my wife!'* The relief and joy was overwhelming and genuine on both sides. I think.

Later, alone, everything caught up with me, a combination of emotions, exhaustion, fatigue and relief resulted in me dissolving into a crumpled heap of tears. Less than impressed at my display, he asked, *'What is wrong with you?'* Not trying to disguise his annoyance, he said, *'If you didn't like it, why didn't you just leave? No one made you stay.'*

Now, I was confused. Flashing past in my head were all the times he had needed to leave a job and had looked to me to understand and back him up, so now, where was his support for me? The conversation was over, he had no more to add: *'It's done, it's over, you don't need to do it again.'* Silenced and afraid of being an eternal drain.

I felt relieved to be away from that big, dirty city and back at the tranquillity of the lake and surrounding countryside, sleeping in my own bed and just being at home. I decided to put it all down to experience, looking at the positives of the extra money I had earned, although I had been expecting some positive feedback having worked my socks off. I had stuck it out in the hope I would be asked to work at a sample sale again. Asking if he had heard anything from his friend, he regarded me with a pained expression. *'I did hear back, but I didn't want to pass it on,'* he said gravely.

Now he had my attention.

'Your comment to that manager didn't go down very well, she was quite offended.' He observed me carefully as I listened to this in complete shock. I began to redden in embarrassment as if I had been caught stealing. *'But I didn't ... we didn't ... nothing was said.'* I rushed my words, not making any sense, as I desperately struggled to remember the conversation. Feeling guilty and ashamed but not really understanding why, I found my voice again. Shaking my head as if in denial, I said, *'We were laughing and joking. I don't understand why she would say that.'* Close to tears of frustration, I looked at him, pleading with him to believe me. Raising his eyebrows, he said, *'Sometimes you have a way of speaking which can come across as brash and rude. I am used to it, so I know you don't really mean it.'* said he continued, *'Maybe it is because you are English, and what is funny to you is not funny to someone else.'*

That was a sobering thought. I knew I sometimes made mistakes even though I was pretty fluent. Maybe my tone was wrong. Something too English, sarcastic. Somehow, in a language I had always felt as comfortable speaking as my own, I had made disrespectful mistakes, upsetting people. This was a sickening realisation.

GASLIGHTING

A MANIPULATION TACTIC SO INSIDIOUS BUT WITH THE SAME END GOAL; TO UNDERMINE WHAT YOU KNOW TO BE TRUE AND FILL YOU WITH DOUBT. ESPECIALLY EFFECTIVE IF YOU ARE ALREADY FEELING UNSURE OR INSECURE. THE OBJECTIVE OF GASLIGHTING IS CONTROL; BY MANIPULATING A SITUATION IN WHICH YOU ARE USUALLY CONFIDENT, A SEED HERE OR THERE OF DOUBT MAY NOT SEEM LIKE MUCH, BUT IF THE CRACKS OF UNCERTAINTY HAVE APPEARED ALREADY, THEN THIS SIMPLY DEEPENS THEM AND WIDENS THEM TILL IT ALL STARTS TO COLLAPSE. TILL YOU START TO COLLAPSE.

I insisted we had enjoyed a friendly conversation, and she had been fine with me. He shrugged his shoulders. *'Well, I have known her for years, and I don't think it is in her nature to make something like that up.'* He smiled at me, saying, *'Not everyone understands your sense of humour.'* Someone I barely knew had possibly misconstrued a three-minute exchange and been offended; it seemed unlikely but possible, I was willing to accept that. Far more shocking was that my brand-new husband had decided to believe them, not me.

It's cold out there on your own, especially when the person you thought most of in the world shuts the door gently but firmly on you.

Chapter 36

Barfly

We lived in a place the rest of the world dreamed of visiting, slap bang on the border between olive tree-filled Umbria and the stunning sweeping conifer-lined hills of Tuscany, like a landscape painting in the richest oils. The lake was so huge it resembled the sea, and its dynamic hues in the ever-changing weather and cloud formations would keep you drawn to the apartment windows, mesmerised by the stunning views. Looking from the outside in, it really was an idyllic setting.

I threw myself wholeheartedly into small-town Italian life, wanting to embrace everything it offered, familiarising myself with the best supermarkets, where to buy decent locally produced wine, marvelling at the still and sparkling mineral water dispenser available to everyone for pennies as long as you brought your own recyclable containers. I was equally impressed with my neighbours, in their seventies and eighties, out in all climates, pruning and maintaining their olive trees, using the discarded branches for firewood while keeping an eye on the precious olives to be turned into liquid gold, keeping them supplied until the next harvest.

Italians, in general, are a fairly suspicious race, and Umbrians, in particular, are known for being insular, initially regarding us with suspicion: Why had we chosen their town to live in? What did we do? Where did we come from? Gradually, we made inroads, breaking down barriers by going to the main restaurant to banter with the staff and to enjoy the wild boar pasta or a pizza to show that we were taking this very seriously; we weren't temporary tourists.

Frequenting the local bars for coffee, we were on first-name terms with many of them. He had set his sights on one particular bar in town right from the get-go. Having talked his way in and offered his front-of-house services on busy weekends and special weekday holidays, it was to me he expanded on his real reason for putting up with the shockingly low pay and inconsistent working times. He had a pipe dream of managing the place himself when the cantankerous owner, who couldn't stand talking or dealing with the general public, would eventually give it up and hand it over, thus allowing him to cast his magic spell over a business he felt in his bones he was born to do.

ENTITLEMENT
CHRONIC NARCISSISTIC ENTITLEMENT IS BASED ENTIRELY ON THE UNIQUE PERCEPTION THAT THEY BELIEVE THEMSELVES TO BE EXCEPTIONALLY EXTRAORDINARY OR EXCEPTIONALLY DEPRIVED (EITHER ONE WORKS); THE WHOLE WORLD OWES THEM, BUT THEY OWE NOTHING IN RETURN—A SIMPLE FACT OF THEIR LIVES.

He was bitingly critical of everything in it, beckoning me inside if I happened to walk past while he was working. Over the heads of the couple he worked for, he gave me sarcastic sideway looks, indicating his repugnance at the numerous ornaments in the bar's dark recesses or the mismatched pictures from the Seventies and Eighties crowding the walls.

'*Look at this,*' he'd say, loudly pointing at dated and bleached-out posters of London landmarks next to an overwhelmingly voluminous bunch of dry and dusty flowers. '*As an English person, you appreciate this, don't you? Isn't it just fantastic?*' he said, grinning at me, involving me in his cat-and-mouse game of taking the piss while looking as if he was charmed. It wasn't just the interior he had issues with. He was caustic about the way the belligerent owner dressed, behaved, spoke (or rather didn't speak), and his inability to plan ahead with even enough bread for incoming crowds, leaving him, my poor beleaguered husband, having to deal with dissatisfied and often hungry customers. *'He just doesn't care,'* he would moan on returning home after his sporadic shifts. *'He shouldn't be allowed to run that place; it is so unfair'.* Was it too much to ask to be allowed to run the place, to be given a chance at making a success of his own business? All he had to do was be his usual gregarious self, charming the customers; after all, he was great at talking to everyone. I could be in the kitchen, churning out an easy, tasty, people-pleasing menu. I could do all that simple stuff standing on my head.

Like those nodding suede dogs everyone had sitting in the backs of their cars once upon a very different time, I agreed. I could learn to work in the kitchen, I thought to myself, glowing with the idea he thought I was that great and that we could work together. I may have been deluding myself, but I quickly learnt never to say out loud that it was a totally bloody ridiculous and selfish idea as the bar wasn't for sale, and even if it was, how the hell would we finance it?

Making the mistake of once talking to him about it honestly had gone down very badly indeed: *'I really don't think they would consider selling it, and I am not entirely sure it would be a particularly great investment,'* I ventured, having heard through the grapevine about the various financial implications of owning a business in such a historic location. *'His wife works for the council, which I am sure has hugely helped them navigate the various rules and regulations,'* I pointed out. It wasn't what he wanted or needed to hear. *'You always do this,'* he yelled at me furiously. *'This is my dream, but you are so negative, you don't want me to be happy, it's always about money for you.'* I considered this and felt he was probably right. I managed the money because he never had any, and now I was so insecure and unsure about finances I had become obsessed, boring myself with it and wrecking my relationship as a result. When exactly had I forgotten how to dream?

To please him, I put my house in France on the market; I didn't need it, as we were never able to go over there, and it would free up the perfect sum of money to start him off in something.

He liked that plan. He liked it a lot.

Chapter 37

How much is that doggie in the window?

In my head, I was convinced that everyone else was more important: their happiness, their comfort, and their desires, and he was very much at the top of the tree. My own joy followed by proxy.

I made sure I always found a way, even if it adversely affected me. Physically, mentally, financially, if you needed it, I would put you, your family, your third cousins and possibly your best mate's sister, first. Sound silly? That's me: exhausted, knackered and frequently worried sick about money but unwilling to ever say no in case it upset someone, feeling a failure if I couldn't make *their* wish come true.

He wanted a dog.

Dogs were expensive and demanding creatures and could be dirty and smelly too. They came with the risk of potentially prohibitive veterinary costs, kennel or boarding fees, astronomical food bills and, unlike children, didn't grow up to become productive family members, paying rent and helping with the housework; they remained needy babies. Their list of requirements was long, and the inevitable expense scared me. I was barely keeping us afloat as it was. In England, it had been out of the question, but his campaign to convince me that having a dog would complete our family was always there in the background. When faced with my reasonable reasons against owning one, he switched and agreed that it was impractical, the time wasn't right, with insufficient money, space or time. He'd nod in thoughtful agreement: *'Yes, it is more expensive here. Maybe one day, when we are back in Italy,'* and I'd be relieved that he had listened and understood. A few days would pass, previous agreements forgotten, and once again, I would have pictures of adorable puppies thrust at me in ads for available litters for sale, feeling like the meanest person in the world as he met my objections with vehement denials he was even looking: *'They appeared on my social media feed, and I was simply showing you.'* I could hardly object to that.

I understood perfectly well he had never really gotten over leaving his beloved dog behind when he moved countries. *'If we had a dog,'* he said, looking at me with sparkling eyes, *'we would be a real family.'* My heartstrings tugged at the thought of the child I was unable to have but the four-legged addition I could. It was such a huge deal, and unwilling to undertake such a massive responsibility from cold, I organised a few dry runs. I took extra house-sitting jobs that involved looking after dogs and signed up as a dogsitter. Dogs of all sizes and breeds would come to stay in our flat for a few days, a weekend or a week. Some were more lovely than others, but I was learning and warming to the idea of having our own. My heart was truly stolen looking after two of the most beautiful, lolloping Great Danes, and sensing weakness, he dived straight in with his 'canine expertise', bombarding me with 'facts' about how Danes were known as 'apartment dogs', ideally suited to smaller living spaces and short walks. He even described them as giant lap dogs!? Not even their food was that expensive, as it was all about knowing what to feed them. Deferring to his superior knowledge, we focused on one day owning our very own Great Dane.

In Italy, he wasted no time at all, spending hours looking for breeders, melting my heart with photos of gorgeous puppies with giant paws. The pricing seemed prohibitive, but I was already hatching a plan to make it happen. His

50th birthday was upcoming, and since we had been together, I had made it my mission to ensure he was always ridiculously spoilt, having told me that birthdays were nothing special in his family, no cakes, definitely no parties, and the idea of presents from his parents was laughable. He had shrugged off my appalled reaction. I was lucky; my family had always taken birthday celebrations seriously. It was lucky, too, for him, that I adored the meticulous planning and organisation that goes into making a special meal, surprise, gift or trip away. I adored surprises, too, but with everyone living in a different country, it would be impossible to plan something like that for me, so the next best thing was to do it for him.

The first part of his birthday present would be the longed-for puppy. After begging for contributions from close friends so we could buy his dream dog, I finally told that, yes, indeed, we could go ahead. A gorgeous harlequin from a renowned breeder in the north arrived, and I was even allowed to name him Buddy after the main character in my favourite Christmas film: *Elf*.

It was not, however, love at first sight for me.

Adorable, obstinate, funny, gorgeous and a huge pain in the backside for the uninitiated. The breeder mentioned him being 'curious'. What a massive, bloody understatement that turned out to be. Whining endlessly at closed doors and needing to know exactly what we were doing and where we were at all times, I found him more than a little overwhelming.

When he first arrived, he was funny and sweet, but he was growing at a rate of knots every day, and I began having serious doubts I could manage. He became unbelievably attached to my new husband, and I stupidly felt like the outsider who didn't know what to do and how to behave. Sensing my apprehension, he offered to return him: *'If you don't want him, I understand,'* he told me gently. *'I know having him is a huge deal.'* I thought about it and wanted to say, *'Yes, please, take him back now, this is way too much responsibility and I feel excluded.'* But I wasn't giving up that easily. To return him because of a wobble would have been cruel.

Regular walks through the town with this beautiful, leggy statement dog attracted admiring glances and adoring the attention the dog drew, he would spend a lot of time engaging with strangers keen to know more. I, too, grew in confidence, teaching him to play games, obey commands and learn to hide and seek in the woods. I cracked up laughing as he 'hid' behind trees with every part of him sticking out, convinced I couldn't see him. His whole raison d'être was to do goofy stuff, and very soon, he became my world.

I had secretly planned a surprise birthday dinner party in a restaurant complete with presents and cake. A group of friends from Rome were all booked into local hotels with instructions to hide in the restaurant. The whole plan worked beautifully, and he delighted in being centre stage; even the cake had a pair of socks and sandals on it. He adored it all—except the presents they had given him!

The people he had known all his life had chosen a selection of beautiful, arty books, several sets of pencils and some lovely drawing books. Receiving them in the restaurant, he made all the right noises and looked delighted, but it was a different story back at home. Turning over the gifts, he examined them all and then dismissed them as unwanted and useless. *'They don't know me at all,'* he complained.

Somewhat surprised at his outburst, I explained that one of them had asked me for ideas, and I hadn't known what to suggest. *'It is a thoughtful gift considering your ability to draw,'* I said optimistically. He looked at me in disgust and said, *'Next time anyone asks you what I want, tell them to buy me decent wine; at least, it will be something I can actually enjoy.'* His disappointment was clear. I could have influenced their choice, but instead, I had let him down. I posted some photos of the weekend on social media, tagging him and everyone who had been a part of the surprise. It took someone else far away to point out what I had missed:

'Why the hell aren't you in any of them?' she asked. I hadn't even noticed.

He hardly looked up from his own phone to say, *'It doesn't mean anything.'* I didn't respond, so he looked up at me irritably, saying, *'Why are you making such a big deal of this? It isn't important, just a few photos.'* Going back to his phone screen, he considered the matter closed.

It hurt.

I was just there to plan and arrange. I wasn't a member of the main cast, I was merely crew. I showed him the photos and the video clips, so obvious now that even he couldn't deny my glaringly obvious absence. *'It makes me feel like I don't count,'* I said. It sounded vaguely pitiful, even to my own ears, but I was really upset and fighting back the tears, angry and frustrated. He looked at me, sighed and then, without stopping for breath, he ranted, *'I knew it was too good to be true, you always find a way to ruin my birthday, every year it is the same and now you are trying to pick an argument over a few silly photographs, you can't ever just let me have a nice time. Thanks very much!'*

There is that ringing again. Ever so slightly louder now.

Chapter 38

Moving On Up

My idea of a better quality of life was not scrabbling around the back of a sofa or in hidden pockets of my bags and jackets for loose change. Cheaper though life was in Italy, it certainly wasn't free, and as my 'ambitious' husband had his eye on the prize of running the local bar, he had to be available to work at a moment's notice if they called him, which they rarely did.

I had to find work, and he agreed.

Searching online for teaching jobs seemed the best option, and I came across a Chinese company looking for teachers with flexible hours and a laptop with a camera. My application was successful, as was the interview and trial lesson, and within days, I started. Advertised as a teaching role, I could have written a better job description to alert potential candidates: *Mother tongue English teachers with additional TV presenter skills needed to entertain and occupy Chinese children of all ages, including bored, insolent teens and toddlers learning to talk*. Setting up a mini office in the spare room with a backdrop of puppets and bright pictures to educate and engage the kids, I threw myself into doing the best I could. The job was knackering and isolating.

Our oversized, attention-deficit Great Dane puppy did not appreciate my need to focus on others. Hating closed doors, he whined and scratched until I let him in, and then he spent his time prowling around, either attempting to steal the visual aid toys or humping the soft furnishings, desperate for me to stop looking at the screen. In the middle of one lesson, while I was busy acting the mimes to 'Head, Shoulders, Knees and Toes' (and bearing in mind every second of each lesson was being recorded for the parents or school to check in on), I managed to discreetly move the screen around with one hand and remove a cushion my dog was trying to have sex with while simultaneously singing tunelessly to the bored child on the screen.

Any complaints I had about the dog needing to be occupied while I was online with the students were quickly shut down. '*I can't teach if he is in the room with me.*' I pleaded, '*Please can you at least make sure he doesn't come in?*' He looked perplexed. '*I have already been out for a walk with him, what else am I supposed to do?*' he said, followed by '*I needed to go to the bathroom, and I didn't realise he had gone in to you. It's not my fault he wants you.*' That was it, there was nothing more to be said, he had done what he could and now the lessons were over, as was this discussion.

The job was relatively well paid, but after months with just the screen for company, I was unhappy; something was missing. We lived in a beautiful place, alive and buzzing with tourists for about five to six months during the long, hot summer season. But it was a freezing, empty ghost town for the rest of the year I craved social interaction with different people in shops, museums, and anything more than in a pizza parlour or on the occasional trip to the supermarket. But I was also annoyed at myself: wasn't this what I had wanted?

No one was unhappier than me with my dissatisfaction. I tried teaching English to the locals just so I could leave the apartment and see real people, but invariably, they were too busy or the times clashed, and walking 500 m to speak basic English wasn't really satisfying my need for some sort of intellectual stimulation.

We made friends with a few people and invited them for dinner, but the return invites eventually petered out; they lived further afield or were busy with their own full and hectic lives. The vintage car we had shipped over was proving to be a bureaucratic nightmare to insure and tax, so we had borrowed an even older car from his parents, which could just about ferry us to the supermarket and back, but neither car was fit for exploring the area.

I was stagnating in a location I appreciated but began to detest because I felt trapped. Working in that closed-off home office was stifling me even more. I rejected suggestions to go for a drive in a car I didn't trust not to pack in suddenly. Was that what it come to? A drive in a car somewhere? Feeling old before my time, like I was growing mouldy from the inside out, made me terribly sad. I was stumped. I didn't know what to do.

The answer arrived unexpectedly in the form of a throw-away comment during a conversation online—a primary school teacher had left, and they needed someone: '*I don't suppose you are interested?*' Yeah, right, I laughed, dismissing the possibility as bonkers. Teach science, English, and history at a bi-lingual primary school in a northern city in Italy? I couldn't possibly. That would be madness, up sticks and move to a city, an industrial hub, no less, a place which definitely didn't fall asleep for half the year.

I couldn't, could I? *We* couldn't—or could we?

I might as well have suggested turning our pet into Sunday lunch. He wasn't so much against the idea as utterly horrified I would even suggest such a crazy notion. It was the first time I had seen him panic. '*Are you out of your mind?*' he yelled at me. '*Why would you even suggest such a ludicrous thing? It is awful up there, horrible and dirty, the people are dreadful, and besides, we have a great life here, a lovely cheap apartment, we don't need to move anywhere else.*'

I replied with a calmness I didn't realise I was capable of: '*I hate teaching online,*' I said. '*I'm alone for hours on end in that room, and even when I am not working, there is nowhere to go and no one to see. I cook dinner and walk the dog. We don't do fun stuff, we never go anywhere, I am bored and tired of it.'*

I took a breath, and before he interrupted, I carried on:

'They have offered me a contract, in an actual school with prospects and a future, there are no jobs here in this bloody place, none for you despite your best efforts. This is an actual career path for me with a contract in a city with stuff to do near the lakes, and I'm sure there will be opportunities for you too.'

The idea of someone in another place offering him proper work didn't appeal.

'WE ARE HAPPY HERE,' he maintained, trying unsuccessfully to keep calm. *'I have been slowly building up trust in that bar, he is close to giving me more work, and you just want me to give that all up, it is always about what YOU want.'*

But I'd had enough; he couldn't maintain us on less than five euros an hour, earned sporadically in a two-bit bar that was empty for seven months of the year, in the vague hope he'd be offered the place to manage because the owner was fed up dealing with the general public. Furthermore, we were definitely NOT happy.

Surprising myself, an excited part of me had woken up, having forgotten she existed. I could feel her uncurling herself from an enforced hibernation, stubbornly resisting attempts to prevent her from a better more exciting life. Feeling her strength seeping into me, I tried explaining what a great opportunity it could be, but he ripped apart arguments of career progression with counterarguments of working in a school closer to where we lived. Why couldn't I just find more lessons in a nearby town? Or keep doing the Chinese thing? Why did I have to ruin everything?

Never once did he suggest that *he* could find work nearby, listing instead all the cons to my pros: more expensive, dirtier, colder, upheaval for Buddy, the apartment where we lived. I tried talking him through the advantages and the opportunities: I had negotiated a flexible four-day week, enabling me to travel back if he preferred to make a go of the bar. We could trial it; nothing was set in stone, I told him. Rather than see it as a compromise for a better future, he angrily told me he had not married me to live separately—a powerful argument, but also horribly ironic considering what was to come.

We returned to my dad's that Christmas. I was exhausted by the endless rows and the disapproving husband who remained upstairs sulking, and with a less-than-festive atmosphere, I carried on regardless. Eventually, my tactful dad, who managed to keep his countenance about the spoilt behaviour of the man-child in his house, took me to one side and made it very clear that I should absolutely do this. It was a fantastic opportunity and a reflection of my capabilities. *'You want more, and you want better,'* he said, *'nothing wrong with that.'*

I accepted the job.

Chapter 39

Foot & Mouth

When I was a kid, whenever I thought of what I wanted to be or do, I had a vivid image of me flying everywhere, dressed smartly with a briefcase in my hand. In my head, I was glamorous, efficient and always busy. For years, my stock response to what I would be when I grew up was always '*Air hostess*' (as they were called in the olden days), never really veering from that.

Growing up, I changed my mind as many times as I had cups of tea, yet that picture was always in my head: me running down the gangway of a plane dressed in a skirt suit and heels, needing to be somewhere important. It was impractical and unlikely, and yet I never quite let go of it.

During my university course, I didn't really know what to do with a couple of languages and an economics degree, and with no real plan, I applied to an Emirates Airlines recruitment advert. The travel aspect particularly appealed, so I felt quietly confident when they called me in for a day of interviews. I would take ten interviews over any exam; the feeling of being chased with a timer for added pressure meant total panic and the inability to collect my thoughts, let alone write anything. Interviews, on the other hand, are a breeze for me. I have zero nerves and no problem articulating who I am or what I want (or they want) to a bunch of strangers.

So there we were, twenty-odd wannabees in the basement of a central London hotel in the middle of the hottest June in decades, all of us dressed up to the nines in smart suits with full faces of makeup. We looked ready to do whatever it took to be employed by this prestigious airline. The interview process took hours as we were tested on team-building, communication and leadership qualities. Split into teams, we spent the day trying to impress and influence the recruitment panel as they followed our progress, writing notes on their clipboards. It's a fine line between standing out, clearly expressing an opinion and demonstrating ability while concealing traits of bossiness, selfishness or lack of confidence. All this while you manage thankless team tasks, including escaping a desert island with the help of a cup and spoon or solving a floor puzzle, which your life depends on as you display the diplomatic skills of Kofi Annan, maintaining inclusivity and leadership skills.

The deviousness required for those job tests makes today's applicants for *The Apprentice* look like children playing shop. Throughout the day, they whittled down the candidates for the final one-to-one interview. We were through, and it was a jubilant feeling as we were finally allowed to change out of the smart suits and heels we had been wearing all day into our cooler, less formal clothes.

Walking confidently and happily into that final interview, the panel of recruiters smiled back and asked how I was feeling: '*So much better now I have changed,*' I grinned, and unable to stop myself, I continued, '*and all that makeup! I'm not used to wearing that much!*' Yes, that was me, Gob Almighty. Having successfully completed seven hours of testing in sweltering heat and getting through to the very last interview, I sat there telling them all how much more comfortable I was makeup-free, wearing a vest top, slouchy trousers and trainers. As the words left my mouth, I knew... and they knew. The world's number-one airline require their staff to remain pristinely 'on duty' until they close their front doors.

Was that a fantasy then? That original snapshot I played over and over in my head? I'm not so sure. Having worked as an office manager running administration teams, starting a cottage industry in the Nicaraguan mountains and an ethical coffee company and travelling between Central America and Europe for years, here I was, living in yet another country and planning a daring move to start over. Intrepid and adventurous and very close to what I had believed in.

Besides, don't all the most successful business people say you need to visualise what it is you want. Focus and it will happen *they* say.

Whoever 'they' might be.

Chapter 40

Life in a Northern Town

My disappearing up north to pursue a career and a better quality of lifestyle left him in a seriously vulnerable position because I gave him a chance to choose.

Understanding his need to remain and be available to work in the hope he would eventually manage the place was what I also wanted for him. I wanted him to pay his rent and me mine; then, after three months, we could re-evaluate. I reassured him, saying, '*Nothing is forever, we could try it and see with no pressure.*' Swallowing his non-existent pride and deciding to let go of his 'dreams', my loving husband put aside his antipathy towards a city he had already decided was scumsville, put on his best face and followed me up there; he had both too much to lose and nothing at all to lose.

It wasn't a romantic, supportive gesture; it was strictly survival.

'*I miss my wife so much,*' he crowed romantically down the phone once I had left to start the term. '*It isn't the same at all for me here alone, no one to play with and Buddy is always looking for you,*' he added, knowing that the idea of being missed would tug at my heart. I encouraged him with talk of new prospects and interesting people, relieved and delighted that he was willing as long as he was with me, so

I set about laying the foundations for this new phase of our lives.

I loved teaching at the school. The class was challenging; the kids had been through several teacher changes, but somehow, I had found my place, and I thrived, and so did they. Despite many parents fearing the school had opted for a desperate last-minute substitute, an English mother tongue speaker who used to work in a coffee shop (Italians have serious selective hearing issues), a grudging respect started to creep in as their children visibly flourished in my classes. I loved being in the city too. The variety of shops and restaurants made me feel like the proverbial country mouse in the big town, walking around wide-eyed at all the new sights, the size of the buildings, the parks and even the traffic. Happily taking it all in, feeling as if I was breathing and living again, I rented a gorgeous apartment in the historic centre with narrow streets and Roman remains close by, which I was optimistic he would approve of, and I couldn't wait for him to join me.

It was amazing when he visited. Excited and proud about my new job and the courage I had demonstrated teaching new subjects successfully, I couldn't wait to take him to the school and proudly introduce him to my colleagues, this missing piece of my life of whom I had spoken so much about. He didn't disappoint, charming them all as they welcomed the handsome husband of their new recruit, reassuring him there was plenty of work available and were more than willing to help him. We wandered around the town hand in hand, ecstatic to be reunited, loving the newness of everything. Feeling validated and relieved, I was filled with confidence we were going to be more than OK. Marriage took time and work and compromise, and while there had been tough times because you can't always agree, we were better and stronger for having pushed through and come out as a team on the other side.

Feelings of optimism and hope for us flooded through me; I loved him and my job, and although the location wasn't in my top ten dream places to live, it certainly offered plenty of scope for creating the foundations of a more stable and secure future for us. A pit stop giving us the helping hand we needed.

Less keen but carefully managing to hide his disgust at being uprooted from his preferred cushty life in the Umbrian countryside and forced to live in a place he despised, he followed me up there, biding his time to punish me for what he felt was the worst decision ever. I wasn't entirely unaware of his dislike of the North. Having lived in Milan years before, he had vilified the people, food, prices and attitudes. His loathing of the suffocatingly grey skies and built-up areas, bad tempers and blatant superiority of a population he believed lived purely to work or had inherited money, allowing them to live as they pleased.

I understood, and up to a point, I agreed with some of the downsides, but this wasn't a big city; it was a big town in the middle of the Italian lake district, and I wasn't asking for a forever ending for the two of us there. I could see the differences having lived in the south, middle and north of Italy, and, as far as I could see, there were pros and cons everywhere. Yes, I missed the wood-burning pizza places, cheap trattorias and laid-back attitude of the southern part of Italy. I also knew we both liked decent holidays, lovely clothes and a beautiful home, and they came at a price. This was a stepping stone to that golden future, and while it may have been more expensive and the food wasn't our favourite, there was plenty to look forward to.

To my absolute joy, several interviews were set up immediately for him, but his feedback after each one was that they weren't really looking for anyone, and he had been seen simply as a favour: '*Quite embarrassing, really,*' he said flatly, walking in the door. '*It was obvious they had nothing for me.*' Pushing aside my own crushing disappointment and feeling mortified for him, I took him out for dinner as a consolation prize, trying to keep his spirits up and puzzled as to why anyone would pretend to raise someone's expectations that way.

Conversely, I loved teaching. Science wasn't something I had ever taught before, but hours of researching online to come up with creative ways of presenting it in the classroom was not a chore because watching those Italian children understand the solar system and build atoms with fluffy balls of wool and wooden sticks, in *English,* gave me a sense of accomplishment and purpose, and I felt genuine pride. In many ways, this made our situation harder because despite loving what I was doing, I felt bad that things weren't happening for him. His praise and flattery of my ability: *'You are amazing, they are very lucky, but they should be doing far more to keep you here'* was a double-edged sword of a compliment (with me walking tensely along the sharp edge of the blade) because his needs were not being met.

In between classes, I hounded the head, the school secretary and even the finance director, pleading with them to honour their promises to help him. I even asked some parents if they knew of anything or anyone who could help. He egged me on, telling me: *'They are all so rich they are bound to have something, ask them as it's in their interests to make sure you stay.'* Feeling less than comfortable requesting anything from these well-heeled virtual strangers, I did it anyway, hoping they might have something he'd be interested in. Yes, *'be interested in'* because it was fast becoming clear he wasn't going to do any old job. We lived in an industrial town; there should have been jobs everywhere. Factory work, however, was not on his radar. Looking horrified, he said, *'I want a job I like, something I enjoy, why should you be the only one liking what you do?'* Very soon, offers of help were replaced with exchanges of looks I was unable to interpret.

Like a magpie picking up shiny objects, he collected people while out walking the dog or simply strolling around town waiting for me to finish. For a while, they would be flavour of the month: *'Not like the other surly envious polentas,'* he'd say, using the regional nickname spitefully, and I would be told how great he/she/they were, how easy to talk to, how well-dressed. Then, as quickly as they had been lauded and praised, they were no longer on his radar because, having served no long-term purpose, they were discarded. Sometimes, he had had work from these acquaintances, a few days in a bar maybe, a month in a restaurant, then, once again, the vitriol began: too rich, too spoilt, too unrealistic, too *northern*. Whatever they had or hadn't done, his scowling expression meant they were no longer to be mentioned.

It was 2018, I was the big five-oh. While no surprise parties were arranged for me or any magical trips away probably because I was so busy at school, instead, the biggest silver lining appeared unexpectedly on the horizon. My house in France sold.

He could certainly pat himself on the back for sticking around.

Chapter 41

Time & Punishment

It was a truly lovely summer. The relief of selling the house was overwhelming. We drove to France to sell anything we couldn't take back in the car to the grateful villagers looking for a bargain. With one week to empty the place we both worked hard and I applauded him on his negotiating and sales techniques, he puffed his chest out, walking taller, delighted with himself.

The sheer bliss of knowing it had all been sorted uplifted us as we leisurely drove back through France and on to Italy, talking about future plans, with the dog lying contentedly on the back seat. Adamant that we needed to move somewhere with a garden for the dog, I half-heartedly agreed with him, mainly because the thought of moving yet again was less than appealing, but Buddy was becoming a handful. My reminders of his previous assurances about Great Danes being relaxed, docile, apartment dogs were disregarded and replaced with concerns and doubts about Buddy's breeding: *'I'm beginning to think he isn't a pure Great Dane,'* he said. The idea that we had been misled upset me, but my priority was the dog and his need for a garden. Thankfully, through a school connection, we were looking into renting something suitable towards the end of the year.

He was also talking to someone about opening a small lunch restaurant in the centre, looking at several sites in the summer. It sounded like a legitimate, genuine opportunity. Finally, he appeared to have found *'his thing'*. My job was secure, and his was about to happen; we were even going away for a proper Christmas holiday break where I could relax on a beach. Everything seemed to be going our way.

Until it wasn't.

He picked me up from school one day, and laughing, full of news, I climbed into the car with stories of the day, gossip about new teachers and my classes. Noticing his downcast expression, I panicked. *'Oh, my god, what's wrong? What's happened?'* I blurted out, thinking of our families, our friends. Shaking his head, he told me that the project for the restaurant had fallen through; there would be no restaurant, no partnership, no managers position. All of his ideas had been a complete waste of time; his running around over the summer to source furniture and look at locations and possible venues had been utterly fruitless. His tone was bitter and his voice low as he said, *'No fucking reason given, no fucking explanation they changed their minds.'*

Undoubtedly, it was a blow, and I really felt for him that day in the car, looking at his defeated face, sad and sorry, because I knew how much he had hoped this would work. The other person had behaved in a duplicitous and cowardly manner. I listened as he ranted furiously about the unfairness of it all, how things like this always happened to him no matter what he did or how hard he tried. Taking a deep breath, I told him that we would find a way through this, that it could have been worse, explaining my initial fear and shock that something had happened to someone close to us. Looking momentarily displeased at my input, he said, *'It might as well have, it's the same sort of thing.'* From that moment on, he didn't bother hiding his dislike or displeasure.

Never one to waste an opportunity to voice his brutal opinions, socialising became both painful and humiliating. No one wants the city they live in to be endlessly knocked, but he managed to work a disparaging remark into every exchange, from my teaching colleagues to the person preparing coffee. The city was officially recognised as one of Italy's most polluted; the terrible air quality was proof of this unfortunate statistic. This fact, he regularly brought up, smiling as he listened out for the opportunity to remind them, particularly if someone had the audacity to mention a beautiful place nearby to visit. He derived an almost superior kick from bad-mouthing their city from stories he had picked up online or heard on the radio about government corruption and landfill full of apparent toxic waste not to mention Mafia connections within local council offices—nasty soundbites, ensuring we weren't invited anywhere, at least not as a couple.

My protestations fell on deaf ears, and a laughing face, *'Oh, c'mon,'* he'd say, *'I was only joking, and these things are true, so if they don't like to hear them, that's hardly my fault. Anyway,'* he continued, *'it isn't as if they are our real friends.'*

The deep shame of it stayed with me because that constant picking and belittling style of negativity wears tissue paper thin, making you feel brittle, tense and defensive.

Chapter 42

The Name Of The Game

There is an Irish expression I grew up with; a frowning, pursed-lipped response to the suspicion that someone close to you might be pulling your leg (a regular occurrence in our large Irish family gatherings): 'Aaaaah, go 'n' bury yer head' was frequently heard around busy kitchen tables groaning with large pots of tea and piles of toast. Not to be confused with burying your head, covering your ears, and totally ignoring the obvious, which is clearly what I appeared to be doing.

Following a full-on week at school, plus private lessons I was unable to refuse crammed into any free' timetable slots, once Friday appeared, all I wanted was a relaxing time at home with a glass of wine and the knowledge I didn't have to be anywhere; hopefully, with time for a few hours lesson planning, so I'd be ahead for the upcoming week. Home, however, was the last place he wanted to be, having spent the week rearranging pantry shelves or pulling apart the hoover to wash the individual parts to pass the time. The expectation was for a day out far away from home *together*. Daring to suggest he took himself off to look at cars (or buy car parts) or visit the shopping centre alone, he was quick to remind me that it was down to me we lived there, and he had been on his own all week, waiting for me; it was incredibly boring and unfair. The unsaid, ever-present accusation lingered beneath his fixed smile: *Don't make this place any harder than it already is.*

I felt like a fucking drain.

Tired, old, miserable and preoccupied with work and fast becoming the biggest party pooper in the world, putting a dampener on every bright idea or adding a dose of domestic reality where it was not wanted – here I am, it's me, the one who ruins everything. According to him, I had always been this way. When we met again after all those years apart, he bought me a T-shirt with the word 'NO!' in large letters printed across the front. Laughing his head off as he gave it to me for Christmas, he said, *'You always say no to everything. Always.'* At the time I shook my head and tried to say it wasn't true, but he told me I was too sensitive, *'It's a joke.'* Not one I found funny because it made me think maybe he was right, and I was the one bringing everyone down, full to the brim of nonsensical responsibilities such as work, the rent, the dog. Why couldn't I just relax and stop worrying and be more spontaneous and relaxed? Like him. *'I just want us to spend some lovely time together, do something normal and get out of this house,'* he pleaded, holding me briefly in his arms.

That crumb of affection saw me agreeing happily to do whatever he wanted, and I would put off any necessary chores, knowing I would ultimately and inevitably pay for my altruistic procrastination. My stress levels steadily increased the longer we were out, with my subconscious tapping away, reminding me I wasn't organised for the upcoming classes or that I didn't have the right equipment for that science assembly. Yet here I was, doing none of that with the start of the week hurtling towards me like an out-of-control train, trying to care less and be more 'him'.

This lack of organisation meant I invariably called him in a panic from school on the Monday, asking him to buy something essential or bring it from home because I had forgotten it. He'd turn up, playing the hero, his eyebrows raised, saying, *'What are we going to do with you?'* Or by leaving the item at reception, my forgetfulness and chaotic methods were soon well known as my helpful husband once again 'saved the day'.

'Comparison is the thief of joy', allegedly, but it didn't stop me from looking at other relationships and wondering why ours was such hard work. A male teacher at my school asked me for recipe ideas to surprise his girlfriend for dinner, another colleague had been spotted romantically holding hands with her husband in a restaurant on a 'date' night, and another spent all week planning their weekends around hiking the nearby mountains with friends, stopping for picnics and beer along the way.

When you love and trust someone implicitly, regardless of any misgivings you may have about their behaviour, it never occurs to you to look at *them* as the possible cause. If your questioning shines a spotlight anywhere near them or at them, they are ready for you, pistol quick with poisonous mockery of others and full of snide criticism for what they consider boring and dull pastimes while subtly encouraging you to become complicit in their derisive ridicule. *'Beer, in this cold place? You must be kidding.'* He grinned at me. *'Can you imagine?!'* Shaking my head, frowning and laughing along, I agreed: *'Of course not, you are absolutely right, it isn't our thing at all, is it?'*

What was *our* thing?

I didn't see *him* as lacking in ideas, hobbies or spontaneity, only myself. Wondering why I carried a perpetual knot of dread in the pit of my stomach when seemingly I had everything I wanted. When love is involved, then there is no room to even consider the other person could be behaving badly or cruelly towards you because that would surely lead to madness.

Chapter 43

Men o' Pause

I was a mess of angry, knackered confusion.

My temper-a-mental (very apt word) body needed an entirely different thought process every single day: how to dress, react, sleep and cope. Spare me, please, those fortunate females who have bypassed the outrageous symptoms this mid-life 'change' throws at the rest of us. I am pretty sure, having been vaguely smug over my lack of periods since having the tumour removed (and let's face it, there wasn't much to be optimistic about at that point), I was now heavily paying the price.

At school, I became adept at hiding my scarlet, sweating face; writing on the blackboard meant I was giving myself time to count down to a facial cooling off while my back was turned to the class. I carried a fan to meetings where I sat tight lipped as any focus on me led to a red-faced meltdown and voicing your opinion in a room full of fresh-faced, smooth skinned teaching staff while you heat up like a dripping mini furnace is not a good look. Even answering my phone lit me up like a Christmas tree, as any emotional change triggered an uncontrollable outpouring of sweat, resulting in inquisitive stares from curious six-year-olds. Manoeuvring through these hormonal pitfalls at school, I looked forward to the love and understanding I was hopeful waited for me at home.

Some women I knew had their husbands researching the menopause online, looking for ways to reassure and comfort their red-faced, unpredicatable wives having recognised the signs. They now worked as a team, united in their quest for the optimum foods to eat and which natural supplements to buy to calm the flushes and soothe the mood fluctuations. I was in awe of their concern and dedication to finding ways not just of re-igniting the intimacy side but their need to guide the women they loved through this minefield of escalating emotions and physical changes.

My husband, on the other hand, harboured no such interest in investigating something he wasn't entirely convinced was genuine. Viewing it as a barrier, literally, to him being able to have the sort of sex life he felt he deserved, he dismissed his input as unnecessary. As far as he was concerned, it was a gross exaggeration used as a label to cover up mental and sexual issues. Doubting my own symptoms, I began to wonder if he could be right. I had been peri-menopausal since they discovered my tumour years ago, and the hot flushes and mood swings had never let up. Was it a physical change, or was I simply a moody, grumpy, unlikeable person? If it wasn't the mid-life 'curse', what was going on with me? I was barely making a show of being happy, but not for lack of trying. Deep down, I knew that if we could share a physical relationship and everything that comes with that, the rest would fall into place. Surely, we could find ways of doing 'it' and even laugh about what didn't work or wasn't comfortable, the natural affection and closeness created in those moments would then be a natural by-product. I wanted this for us. I missed the physical side of things and was prepared to work at it in any way possible.

Instead, I was held at an invisible arm's length, useful for some things but not quite enough to be on his ride.

Since chemo, sex had been painful for me, so feeling entirely at fault, I looked for creams, pessaries, even tablets, anything to *smooth* the way. Aware I didn't work properly but realising my mood swings and hot flushes were 'a thing', he told me we definitely weren't in this together as it was a *female* matter. Any objections from me to this blatantly sexist attitude, and I was reminded of how much he was already doing in the face of my hysterical screaming hormones: *'When you are always in such a bad mood, I don't rise to it, I wake each morning feeling happy and positive,'* he explained as if spelling out the obvious to a petulant child. *'You are always so angry in the morning, it makes it very hard for me.'* This zen-like calm he claimed to have the monopoly on evaporated during arguments; he had no qualms about viciously throwing in my face my failing, as his wife, to provide a basic staple of the marriage: impromptu sex, something which was as vital to him as food. *'I have a physical need as a man,'* he raged, uninterested in the idea that I also wanted it but didn't fancy being ripped apart.

Feeling shame at my lack of a 'normal' functioning body, I wondered how to rekindle that affection; it seemed to have been entirely replaced by a huggy, back-slapping, fraternal-style friendship, making me feel less and less attractive. His moves on me were not because he liked my body or found me desirable; it felt juvenile, jokey, which is exactly how I felt, a bit of a joke. In public, he automatically took my hand, but it felt mechanical rather than an actual need to hold a part of me. If I ever dressed up in clothes he considered sexy, he walked towards me, staring fixedly and clamping his top teeth over his bottom lip, reaching out to grope or paw a part of my body, making grunting noises.

As a seduction technique, it needed work.

Did it make me feel sexy? Wanted? Desired? No! I recoiled from these sorts of advances, feeling like the ultimate failure. Desperate for the closeness of a physical relationship, I tried explaining what might help me 'feel more receptive', but he shut me down, groaning, *'It loses all spontaneity if you have to spell it out like a lesson.'* Seeing his disgust and detachment, humiliated misery washed over me, and I retreated, feeling myself shrivel up even more.

My confusion at what was 'wrong' with me was exacerbated by how different I was perceived at work. I coped with teaching several different year groups; my colleagues told me how envious they were of me being tall and slim, compliments abounded from staff and parents on my 'cool' clothes and my teaching abilities. Dreaming up dynamic projects to engage the children, motivated by the laughs I had with close colleagues and a blissful feeling of being needed and valuable was the professional environment I thrived in, until it was time to leave. Tired but satisfied, walking out of that building, my spirits started fading, and the dimmer switch on my lightness turned to low as I walked or cycled back home.

Within seconds of opening the door, I felt his mood and mindset and knew whether to be lively and chat or withhold stories of my day. Feeling guilty for any happiness or fun I may have experienced at my job, I switched that light right down to avoid shining and highlighting his own dull and boring day. My questions were met with a caustic reply: *'What do you think I've done all day by myself, except wait for you?'* So, retreating, afraid to speak because it felt like showing off, I unknowingly created my very own invisibility cloak.

The trouble with hiding who you really are is that you might end up drowning in that forced silence.

Was this the menopause, or was I just plain miserable for fear of doing the wrong thing? I no longer knew if I needed a hug, a shag, a working husband or just an extra-large bar of Dairy Milk. Had I become 'the man' in this less-than-emancipated relationship? Taking on responsibility for almost everything, maybe I had become both the man and the woman.

Brilliant, I had become asexual. In an ever-changing world of being whatever we want to be, I was certainly in fashion.

Chapter 44

Rose-Tinted Sunglasses

Spring came as a welcome relief in 2019. I used the hot weather as a reason for my sudden high colour or need to speedily open a window during a lesson to let in some deliciously cool air. *'Gosh, isn't it warm today?'* I exclaimed to the children, busy working on their bids to become class president. Meanwhile, at home, I was dealing with another equally determined manifesto: my husband had now decided that his only chance at employment was on another continent.

Africa.

On what planet did I believe he needed to travel 5000 miles away from me to work in a bar? As an intelligent woman with a myriad of qualifications and social and language skills, did it not once occur to me how weird it was that a grown man who has been living back in his own country for almost three years with a smattering of English was unable to find any consistent work?

Yes, it certainly did. But he was ready for any scepticism or reservations I had, skilfully batting away my doubts with plausible explanations replete with promises about a rosy future, sunshine and possibilities. Reminding myself of the efforts he had made, but through no fault of his own, had been let down by one dismal person after another, I felt for him. Poor bloke, nothing was his fault, and I was so very lucky to be in a job I loved. All he wanted was the same, and he was willing to travel to a place he had loved many years ago on holiday. This in itself surely redefined his tenacity and willingness to work.

He also had a clever way of turning it back round to me: *'Well, if I don't go, what shall I do?'* he asked. *'You tell me what the answer is. I am doing my best here.'*

Feeling guilty for dragging him to an area where there was no work, I wholeheartedly endorsed his move.

> **PLAYING THE VICTIM**
> A NIFTY LITTLE TOOL USED BY NARCISSISTS TO JUSTIFY ABUSE OR MANIPULATE OTHERS. BROADLY SPEAKING, IT MEANS AVOIDING ACCOUNTABILITY, GAINING SYMPATHY AND INFLICTING GUILT WHILE AT THE SAME TIME LOOKING LIKE AN INNOCENT CHILD.

My ability to sell snow to Eskimos, as my mother had once described my persuasion techniques, now truly came into its own. When I mentioned the news my husband was leaving me for a work opportunity in Kenya, I was widely regarded with disbelief, wide-eyed amazement and tight-lipped confusion as I nonchalantly defended his choice. If anything, I was irritated by the lack of understanding (had he been offered something where we lived, he would have stayed put), my unwavering support evident in the shrugging of my shoulders and more than slightly resentful towards the invisible forces who had held back this pillar of work ethic.

In my head, I don't believe I thought much past making him happy. I'd move to Africa if necessary and work in a school over there, diversify. I always had and would do whatever it took. My main objective was to ensure he had every opportunity and possibility, allowing him to pursue his dream. And if it didn't work? We were a team and could cross that eventual bridge if and when it happened.

The time I spent alone while he was away wasn't easy on a practical level: back and forth to lessons, escaping with limited time to feed Buddy, making sure he wasn't on his own for too long, collapsing into bed every night, shattered but somehow less stressed. I missed him, but I was determined to take advantage of this time apart and create a new 'me', an improved version of this spiky, moody, work-obsessed harridan he had been dealing with.

It didn't work out for him in Africa.

He returned after an extended stay of approximately six weeks, disappointed and maybe a teeny bit humiliated. Showing off my most loving and patient side, I went out of my way to console and reassure him: *'You gave it a go!'* I said. *'That was amazingly brave. It wasn't your fault there was nothing out there.'* I was angry at his so-called friend who had led him very much up an expensive and distant garden path.

He could sign up for something to do with graphic design. In Milan, maybe? A training course giving him those all-important qualifications, a step up into a career. *'You have so much creative talent, it could be exactly the right thing for you,'* I lovingly explained, proud of my brainwave to set him up. Agreeing wholeheartedly with everything I was saying, he looked sad and dejected, having once again fallen victim to someone else's lies. I felt sorry for him, but proving my faith in him and giving him the means and space to pursue his dream was, in my mind, a positive thing. He knew I had his back, no recriminations, we were in this together, and I was suitably proud of the new calmer me.

I was blissfully unaware that my moods had nothing to do with *his* future plans because while appearing genuinely receptive to my suggestions, he had worked out his own plan to leave as soon as possible.

Chapter 45

It's definitely you me

He was off to Rome.

Networking with a family he assured me were 'serious' people. As friends of friends connected to his past, they came with a metaphorical stamp of authenticity: the brother, who had several businesses, and his adorable sister, whom he had vaguely known when he was younger, and were now doing everything they could to find him the sort of work he deserved—genuine, reliable contacts—unlike those in the north.

Stuck in my own personal catch-22, I understood his need to find work, but I was disappointed that my shiny, relaxed persona had made no difference and no matter what I did, I continually failed.

The comments started innocently enough. Looking at Buddy, he told me I was spoiling him: *'Stop giving him treats, he is far too fat.'* I was left feeling undermined and insecure about what was best for him. Going to tremendous efforts with a favourite meal, he looked puzzled: *'I don't know what it is,'* he said while chewing the spare ribs he usually adored, *'but they just don't taste as good as the last time.'* Dressing up to go out, he'd look at my clothes: *'That? Again?'* and defending the dress he had always loved on me, he simply remarked, *'Yeah, I know I like it.*

I've just seen it a million times. You have so many clothes, it would be good to see you wear something different.'

> **DEVALUE**
> WHEN THE DYNAMICS OF THE RELATIONSHIP START TO SHIFT DRAMATICALLY, AND THE PREVIOUS INTENSE AFFECTION AND POSITIVE ATTENTION GIVES WAY TO FAR MORE NEGATIVE BEHAVIOUR. OR WHEN SOMEONE MAKES YOU FEEL LIKE SHIT FOR NO TANGIBLE REASON, EXCEPT THEY CAN AND DO WHILE SMILING SO THERE IS NO COMEBACK.

Nothing was ever 'meant nastily', and if I dared defend myself, asking what he had to be so critical about, he'd be staggered, shocked even. Turning it back onto me, he would ask in a voice taught with hurt and anger: *'What is actually wrong with you? I only said it as a constructive comment. Am I no longer allowed an opinion?'* Taken out of context, it did feel like the most stupid thing in the world. He loved me. When had I become so sensitive? So ridiculously touchy?

Calmly and slowly, as if speaking to someone with learning difficulties, he tried to explain: *'You really need to talk to someone as the pills aren't working.'* Seeing my confused reaction as I wasn't and had never been on any medication, I tried protesting, but he would patiently insist: *'Perhaps then you need something strong as you need help. I can't help you, I have tried my best.'* Then, looking at my tear-stricken face, he would sigh at my inability to understand what was so evident to him, and continuing in a low voice (which only served to showcase my own growing hysteria), he told me: *'People are scared to say what they think to you, you fight with everyone until they just walk away, tired of you.'*

The soft verbal equivalent of being body slammed.

It's hard enough articulating feelings you don't understand in your own language; in another, it's like trying to speak with your mouth taped up, especially if the person you are desperately trying to communicate with talks faster and louder. It doesn't matter how good your language skills are; if you aren't being heard you shout louder especially when all your explanations are washed away in loud poisonous accusations. Seeing me lose my temper was all the validation he needed as he backed away into the corner of the room, holding his arms up, willing my clenched fists to push at him, but ashamed of my temper, I removed myself when the outpouring of venom prohibited any sort of conversation.

Hiding in the bathroom when I could feel myself losing it, sobbing and willing myself to calm down, I'd hear a soft knock on the door, gentle, forgiving words coaxing me out and telling me he didn't want to fight, just to hold me, everything I wanted and needed to hear from my darling husband, my beautiful soulmate, who had always been there telling me how much he loved me, on the other side of the door.

I was no good to him locked away upset, frightened and reflecting on the verbal vitriol we had just exchanged. He needed me shouting and angry in full battle stance right in front of him so he could talk over me, explaining that I was no longer the person I once was, that my aggressive character and desperate need to be in control had rendered me unlovable, that I couldn't keep blaming hormones, cancer or death in the family because the truth was there was something very wrong with me.

'I just want the woman I fell in love with, I don't know this person anymore,' he whispered, and opening the door to his pleas, feeling wrung out and empty, I let him wrap his arms around me. The relief was intense because, evidently, I *was* hostile, unreasonable and antagonistic. I listened as he explained what it was like to be around me: I picked and picked at tiny insignificant issues until they became bigger because I relished arguing, my goal achieved when we dissolved into shouting and ranting.

Sighing, he looked directly at me: *'All I want is a quiet life.'* Looking at this kindly-eyed gentle giant, I wondered what had happened to me. How had I alienated everyone?

I clung to him, thanking my lucky stars – the only one who had stuck by me and understood – it didn't matter where he needed to go, I had to support him just as he had always supported me—the nightmare who was his wife.

Chapter 46

Viral

In late December 2019, I was struck down by the worst flu ever. A sky-high temperature no medication could touch, agonising headache and a racking cough. The doctor was concerned enough to organise a scan to check for pneumonia. Luckily, I only had severe bronchitis, and despite a longer recovery time, I never gave it another thought.

Until nearly three months later.

I wasn't the only fashionably early one. In my school of 110 kids, 55 were off sick with high temperatures and coughs. All too familiar now, but back then, it was merely a topic in class, This new virus in China, terrible, but as far away as the country itself. The idea that we were living in the European epicentre of an (as yet) unconfirmed worldwide pandemic wasn't just unlikely, it was implausible.

**

I had already been having quite the time of it at school, dealing with a parent who was trying his ignorant best to create problems for me. His 'interesting' parenting skills centred around his own desire for his ten-year-old to grow up quickly so he could be a sexual trailblazer amongst his peers and make his daddy proud. He held me personally responsible for the discipline and education I enforced in the classroom, and any shortcomings his child had were down to me. No completed homework? Can't spell or read? Difficulty following the simplest instructions? Must be the teacher.

That ol' chestnut.

I kept up a brave face at school because I had no choice; payment of fees were the priority rather than the welfare of their staff. At home, I crumpled a little and called him. *'It's not fair,'* he whined. *'Always problems when I am away, and I can't help.'* I'd find myself soothing and reassuring him that everything would be fine, and I could and would cope until our forthcoming mini break planned at the beach place. Already in the capital awaiting another definite interview, we were to meet there and then drive down together.

Covid-19 was about to blindside us all.

The mass exodus of those living in northern Italy to families in the south happened in early March of 2020. The world looked on incredulously – well, maybe not China, as they had problems of their own. Italians are not the best in a crisis, but in a health crisis, their stress levels literally skyrocket, and trains from the virus-struck north carried thousands of Italian migrant workers down to the (briefly) virus-free south. Watching the surreal events unfold online, I worried myself stupid about finding a way back up for the start of school as motorways, borders and towns were closed and policed to stop those without residences or permits from getting through. It didn't seem real, and yet the lines of ambulances and lorries packed with bodies for mass burial were undeniable.

As everything in the country came to a shuddering stop, his primary feelings were fury that his chance at employment was once again ruined. With no sympathy for the escalating mortality rate across the north, he declared they only had themselves to blame for living in such a polluted area, rendering them more susceptible to illness. His anger was directed instead at the personal injustice—his own work prospects delayed by a burgeoning world pandemic.

> **LACK OF EMPATHY**
> A DEFINING CHARACTERISTIC OF A NARCISSIST. ANYONE FACING SADNESS OR PAIN IS IRRELEVANT, AND THEY COULD CARE LESS UNLESS, OF COURSE, IT IMPACTS THEIR OWN LIVES IN WHICH CASE IT IS A SOURCE OF DEEP IRRITATION. THE ABILITY TO FAKE EMPATHY WORKS WELL AS A SELF-SERVING MANIPULATION TOOL BUT ULTIMATELY IS IMPOSSIBLE TO MAINTAIN.

I was preoccupied looking for train tickets, worrying myself silly I'd miss the start of term, regardless of whether the school would be opening or not. Everyone was holding their breath waiting for instructions from a government who themselves had been thrown into confusion. He, meanwhile, switched the rhetoric according to whatever he found on social media, from claiming it was a storm in a teacup to dismissing it as highly unlikely it would ever reach the south. I was no doctor, but packed trains full of infectious people travelling through Italy was not the best method to contain it to one region. Keeping my opinions to myself, his panic at the prospect of returning alongside his wife was palpable.

After successfully finding a train ticket, I looked at him and asked, '*Are you coming with me?*' Frowning and squeezing his lip between his fingertips, he looked as if he was genuinely considering his options. '*I want to come with you, but what if I have an interview?*' He let me make the decision for him. '*No, of course, that wouldn't be right, you need to stay here,*' I said, waiting and hoping he would insist on coming with me. He smiled regretfully and said, '*You couldn't make it up, could you?*'

I murmured in agreement.

Despite him berating it as a terrible and personal inconvenience, Covid had just handed him a metaphorical key to lock me up far away while giving him the freedom he required *and* the perfect excuse not to work.

Chapter 47

Before

Lockdown happened.

Not usually known for its leadership qualities, Italy's decision to shut the country down invoked initial disbelief and then – slowly, like the virus, as people caught on or caught *it*, the rest of Europe followed suit, sneezing in solidarity behind closed doors and deathly quiet streets.

A safe 600 km away, the love of my life frequently called me to describe the hard-knock living conditions in that cold makeshift property on the beach. When I suggested he drove up to be with me and all the home comforts he could wish for as the entire country closed, he said, '*I really wish I could, but it makes more sense for me to stay here.*' With no networking or interview excuses, his needs were altogether more basic: '*I prefer to be by the sea, I would go mad up there with nothing to do and you busy all day.*'

I missed him, but our ferocious rows were not a distant memory; they were painfully carved out in my mind and still smarting. Reluctant to blame him, as I felt I was the volatile and highly-strung protagonist in those dreadful scenes, I welcomed the distance. The idea of him having to cope with my erratic mood swings while being under 'house arrest' in a place he hated was inconceivable – an extra burden I didn't need in that moment. Besides, the real reason for not kicking off at his absence was far more compelling: I truly believed it would be over very quickly, and things would be back to normal. He wholeheartedly endorsed this theory and sprinkled our conversations with effusive and elaborate promises about the future.

I congratulated myself on being so open-minded and having such a wonderful, trusting relationship.

I didn't spend those long, lonely hours creating chewy sourdough or throwing pottery shapes with Amazon starter kits because, as a teacher, I was up to my bloody neck in online lessons. Every waking moment was spent creating history and science homework videos, between caring for the dog and shopping excursions within the recommended curfews. I juggled endless teacher Zoom meetings. Each morning, I maintained the attention of a dozen children as they sporadically showed up in *Celebrity Square*-style windows on a screen, in different states of undress or between mouthfuls of breakfast.

It didn't stop with the lessons; the parents also needed babysitting. One call after the other of one-sided laments long and painful enough to make your ears bleed. If he detected any vulnerability or angst about the scale of my job list, he highlighted my good fortune at having something to do, a warm apartment, the dog for company and money. To counteract his discomfort (and my guilt), I sent funds, an electric blanket, a radio, and, as the weather warmed up, lighter clothes, anything to alleviate his lonely discomfort.

With no end-of-year school play, I felt sad my year 5s were missing out on their final year of primary school celebrations. With the help of another teacher, we came up with the idea of an actual physical book full of stories written by them. Incorporating a competition to involve another year group, we decided the best one would be used as the cover. And who better to illustrate their stories? Thinking of how to encompass his love of drawing into something he could be involved with and occupy his days which could even turn out to be lucrative—his name in print no less! I was full of optimism, hope and pride because I knew how talented he was.

Demonstrating an initial enthusiasm for the project, I duly sent him details of the characters and storylines, leaving the design up to him. The first few he sent through were wonderful, but very quickly, he lost interest, and several were hurried, scribbled, irrelevant sketches. Now we were bickering about this, and I could feel a burning resentment rising; he had agreed, yet here I was *nagging* him. Once completed, the shine had been well and truly removed by his reluctance to finish them.

I was also baffled as to why and where he kept disappearing to.

He regularly drove into Rome to see his friends despite police-controlled road blocks. Never one to follow the rules, he had maintained the same (Roman) address on his license, giving him free access to the city he no longer lived in. '*Lucky friends,*' I said sardonically, feeling the pinch of isolation and loneliness. '*It is literally less than an hour away,*' he'd snap (while I was at least five). '*I haven't seen anyone for ages,*' he'd say, justifying himself, and I'd agree, feeling mean and selfish that I was feeling excluded. '*Yes of course, you must go, you deserve some company.*'

If I asked (any) questions about who he was seeing or why he was there, he'd swerve those pesky interfering intrusions into his way of life by changing the subject, or the conversation would become convoluted about cars or traffic or people he needed to meet. Too much interest from me resulted in him abruptly terminating the call.

WORD SALAD
THERE'S NOTHING HEALTHY ABOUT THIS. IT'S A COVER-UP CONVERSATION IN THE EVENT A SUBJECT NEEDS CHANGING. TOSS A LOAD OF WORDS INTO A VERBAL MIX, NONE OF WHICH MAKE SENSE, END IT, AND THEN RESUME LATER WHEN THE OTHER PERSON CAN'T QUITE REMEMBER WHAT THE ORIGINAL TOPIC WAS, OR PERHAPS YOU 'MISUNDERSTOOD'. EXHAUSTED, YOU GIVE UP. GENIUS AND DEVIOUS.

The weeks turned into months, and although the single sound of ambulance sirens had somewhat subsided, the speed of my invisible treadmill hadn't slowed down and lockdown was starting to take a serious toll on me. I changed mirrors, rugs, sofas and chairs around in the flat, anything for a different perspective. With restrictions gradually relaxing, I started hiking with a colleague from school who could barely conceal her surprise I was still alone.

Justifications to remain where he was regarding the possibility of work sounded hollow and vague to both of us. *'It's not acceptable,'* I told him, *'I need you here.'* Nearly three months had passed, *'I'm losing it,'* I said, only half joking, hoping he would pick up on my frazzled state of mind. A last-ditch attempt at remaining down there – he insisted he needed new tyres – managed to cast a shadow on his imminent return. *'Don't bother coming back,'* I told him furiously. Sensing a fraying of the elastic he had pulled so tightly, he immediately became conciliatory: *'No, no, my love, I was only worried about the long journey, I can sort them another time. You are my wife, and I really want to come home, I am desperate to see you, I am on my way.'*

The front of my stupidly optimistic head was filled with hopes for an emotional, sexy reunion, and after our initial hug, he held me at arm's length and said, *'Oh, you don't look half as bad as I was expecting.'*

Welcome home, darling!

The delight at seeing his dog was genuine and reciprocated; a welcome distraction for me at least as I navigated my way shyly around the apartment which for months had been so familiar and now with the presence of someone else felt strangely different. Clocking the changes I'd made with furnishings and plants, he nodded or said nothing. He felt like a stranger with me waiting on his approval, a disconnected mismatch. Perhaps we just needed a few days to become used to each other?

His disdain at being back in a place he despised was blatant, and his hatred and spite towards everything and everyone he encountered was merciless. Unable to talk about school because his lip would curl at the mere mention of the place he considered had let him down so badly, I barely mentioned it. Nothing interested him and everything and everyone was judged and criticised and reviled with a bile so intense it frightened me. The misery leached from my pores, and I no longer had the resources to plaster over his bitterness. His dismissive response to my unhappiness was borderline cruel: *'I came back, didn't I?'*

Credit where credit's due; it takes a special sort of person to make the one you supposedly love the most desperately crave time *alone* after nearly twelve weeks apart.

Something was starting to shift in me, and I felt an anger simmering for reasons I couldn't quite identify. Realising his usual diversion techniques of initiating arguments based on my numerous failings were no longer working. He changed direction and became caring and concerned for my well-being. *'You are so right, my love, you* do *need a break. I will drive you down to the beach house and let you have some time on your own by the sea – it is your turn for a change of scene and some time out to recharge.'*

Exactly the right words at precisely the right time, but I wasn't entirely fooled. Worn down and out by his nonstop malice, the elastic had well and truly snapped; the beach house on my own sounded like the balm I needed. Having sorted the dog sitter, we set off, barely speaking on the long journey south. My stomach was tight, and I fought to hold back the tears, looking out into the dark as I relived the previous solitary months, what I had endured, and how I had nothing left to give. Arriving late at night, he insisted on parking in the courtyard; quite why he needed to hide the car inside that tiny space was beyond me, but too tired and upset to care, I headed to bed, my back rigid with tension.

Actions speak louder than words, but zero action screams the loudest if only I had been listening. After lying awake all night, I painfully concluded that, as long as I provided, he never would. Uneasy and apprehensive, I waited for him to wake up.

Quietly but firmly, I told him to go. Where to, I no longer cared, but I didn't want him near me. He was aghast. Having successfully left the north he had no intention of going anywhere else, and his promises made to me were as empty as his mouth, which now fell open.

'What about MY holiday?' he whined.

I looked at him, frowning slightly, and softly said, *'Your fucking holiday?'*

Giving me time to 'calm down', he left and returned after twenty minutes, surprised to find I hadn't changed my mind. *'Where am I supposed to go?'* he asked. *'I don't have any money, not even for fuel to Rome.'* His tone was petulant, but saying nothing, I emptied my purse into his hand and walked back inside.

Chapter 48

During

I hadn't given up on us; even as I closed the gate that day, some part of me still loved him and hoped that being cruel to be kind would work, and he would step up and show me I wasn't wrong.

Admitting as much to my dad when we spoke, he agreed totally, saying no matter how difficult it feels, a marriage or any serious relationship takes commitment, compromise and guts, fully supporting me on the idea that pushing him out of his 'comfort zone' was the right move. I spoke to sceptical friends who had heard it all before. I had been frustrated in the past, but this time, I was unflinching as I knew I couldn't go on like this. *'Where is he?'* they asked, but I had no idea, numb at the state of my marriage.

I missed my dad so much. I had been unable to see him since Christmas because rules were rules, and he was a stickler for them. Our phone calls were regular and long, and we updated each other on everything from the pandemic to politics to plant care, although I would have given anything to stand in his garden and talk to him, see him laugh and cook him a Sunday roast. Continued limitations on travel to the UK and his absolute belief that he needed to isolate meant phone-calls were all we had.

In the meantime, I was being inundated with loving messages full of promises from *him*. Refusing point-blank to live without me as I was his '*everything*', he now realised I had been through too much and wanted to make it up to me. Excited and optimistic, he had a job using his English, and in between, he was busy driving his sick mother to and from the hospital. He even had a female friend call me to tell me how much he loved me and I shouldn't give up on him. So many seemingly believed in him, in us.

Had we finally turned a corner? I started to soften. To believe. To hope.

> **HOOVERING** *COMBINED WITH* **LOVE BOMBING,** *WITH A TINY TASTE OF* **TRIANGULATION.**
> LET ME BREAK IT DOWN; THE FIRST TWO ARE EXACTLY AS THEY SOUND – AN ONSLAUGHT OF TACTICS USED TO ENTICE YOU BACK SHOULD YOU BE CONSIDERING THAT THE RELATIONSHIP IS NOT EXACTLY WHAT YOU WANT/NEED/IMAGINED, SO SUCKING YOU BACK IN WITH THE FORCE OF A BLACK HOLE, THROWING EVERYTHING YOU HAVE ASKED FOR IN YOUR DIRECTION. IN THE EVENT YOU ARE RETICENT AND STILL UNSURE THEN SOMEONE ELSE IS ADDED TO VALIDATE THEIR CLAIMS AND PERSUADE YOU – DEMONSTRATING WHO IS IN CONTROL.

Seeing him trying his best, I demonstrated willingness too. Having rented out his beach place for August, I suggested we use the money to go away somewhere neutral and talk properly, taking it one day at a time. He could not have been more delighted at the prospect of a holiday in the sun, whereas I looked at it as couples therapy, an opportunity for us both to understand why we had reached breaking point and how to make sure it never happened again.

That holiday felt as brittle as our relationship, with no intimacy, no physical closeness because, as far as he was concerned, he had a job now which cancelled everything else. My persistence in trying to find out why we had broken down was a source of exasperation for him, and his lack of accountability for the state of our marriage breathtaking. On the days we did manage to be friendly, I couldn't quite shake the feeling that something unidentifiable felt very false, as if he was biding his time.

The day before flying back from Greece, I received a call.

My dad had died.

Chapter 49

After

When someone you love dies, it is shocking.

Whatever the circumstances or age, even with an expected death, the impact is immediate and paralysing, making it hard to absorb much of what is going on around you. Moments of normality and rationality come and go, enabling you to fleetingly forget what is actually happening. Then you remember, and the pain is a piercing, physical assault.

I was lost, needing reassurance and support, a rock I could depend on. Someone in Rome he knew found and paid for a ticket back to the UK; unexpectedly, I was inundated with messages on social media from well-meaning people I barely knew offering condolences less than a day after I had heard the news. This was more than I was ready to deal with, but he appeared bewildered that I wasn't more grateful for the well-meaning broadcast. He was just trying to make me feel better, this slippery rock of mine.

At the funeral, he held my hand and played the role of the dutiful and caring husband, leaving soon after to wait for me back in Italy while the pieces of a house now empty of parents were sorted. Eventually returning, it very much felt as if my grieving should have finished. Life goes on. I was taken to one side by the school and told (in a mask-wearing environment) that I should make an effort and smile more as my sadness was being picked up by the children I was teaching, and parents were complaining.

Cheer up.

The shine of being a provider had worn off for him, too, and his imminent return to Rome was making me nervous at the thought of being alone again. Covering it up like a good 'un, I gave him money to make his life easier. I wanted him to find a decent builder because I was willing to invest in the beach house to create a proper home. I tentatively suggested he took Buddy with him, explaining how tough it would be driving back and forth between lessons. His crestfallen face told me everything: *'I'd love to, but it wouldn't be fair on him.'* I tried to say that if he was working shifts, he'd be at home a lot more than I would, but talking over me, he protested, *'I have no idea where I will be or my hours. I would prefer it if he was here... to protect you.'*

Game, set, and match to him while I was left wondering how I was going to fit it all in.

Chapter 50

Enough is Enough

In the summer, on any beach in the world, you will find this same scene: a small child happily clutching a bucket, pootling down and back to the shoreline, collecting seawater for their sandcastle. Utterly convinced of their ability to fill that moat.

I could relate to those children; my own energy and time were being absorbed while nothing changed, and now, I was waking up to the fact that I was seriously struggling on all fronts. The one person who had been the embodiment of all that was right in my world, who had grounded and encouraged me not just as a moral compass but as a guiding, loving, one had gone forever. It was becoming clear that no matter how many buckets I filled the sandcastle was about to collapse.

He returned to Rome. I cheerfully waved him off, hiding the hole in my heart, not wanting to cling on but desperately needing to be held.. .Reassuring me with amazing potential prospects, all *I* needed to do was finish this school year. We had been separated before, and we could do it again.

'Of course, I will miss you, but the time will pass quickly,' he told me, one foot already out the door, *'then we can be together again.'* He smiled, looking at his watch.

'*Maybe Christmas somewhere?*' I asked pathetically, and he nodded absent-mindedly.

> **FUTURE FAKING**
> PART OF THEIR MANIPULATION CURRICULUM—IT HAS NOTHING TO DO WITH THE FUTURE BUT EVERYTHING TO DO WITH THE HERE AND NOW, SAYING WHATEVER NEEDS TO BE SAID OR PROMISED TO FULFILL THEIR OWN IMMEDIATE NEEDS AND DESIRES. STRINGING YOU ALONG, BASICALLY.

Finding moments to call me, he always sounded happy, and I badly wanted to share in his carefree attitude instead of feeling like the sky was falling in on me. Less than overjoyed to hear any sort of negativity, he often cut short our conversations, citing work or meeting commitments, ending the calls and leaving me to my state of perpetual worry about a demanding school timetable and spiralling costs in an apartment where my salary was being consumed at a rate of knots. Discovering I had paid an electricity bill for myself and two other apartments in the building I had lived in for nearly two years was quite something. The evidence notwithstanding, my claims to the family who owned the entire property were summarily dismissed as inconsequential, and they subsequently sent nasty legal letters demanding a deposit never previously required.

This was the final push I needed; I wanted out.

The truth is I really wanted what he seemed to have down there, what I heard in his voice before he remembered to tell me how tired he was or how long his hours were. I wanted a piece of that freedom and joy. Deep inside, I no longer wanted to manage and cope; instead, I wanted to eat well, smell the sea air and sleep; more than anything I wanted to sleep, because every part of me felt so damned exhausted. I needed the luxury of just stopping.

He was less keen at my news of joining him and tried his utmost to dissuade me, listing reasons why it wasn't quite the right time: the work had started at the beach house, so he would need to find somewhere for two people, it wasn't easy to rent a place, he was alone so could stay at friends' houses and could I not at least finish the school year, stay until Christmas? Soothing my stubborn protestations with talk of not wanting me to lose any money the school owed me if I left early, he advised, '*After all you have done they need to pay you, if you leave mid-term, you will lose that. Perhaps the doctors will sign you off?*' A *friend* of his had advised him I should declare mental stress as the cause.

He hit the nail on the head with that one. I was extremely concerned I was letting people down by leaving the school, and I also worried that my dad wouldn't have approved, but knowing him as well as I did, I imagined he would want what was best for me. For the fourth time in nine years, I packed up alone and moved out.

Driving away from that dank, foggy, polluted northern town in my little car, tightly packed with belongings I couldn't bear to sell or leave behind, I started to breathe again. With the radio up full blast, I shouted along optimistically to the chorus as I pelted down the motorway through Italy: Jess Glynne, 'Hold My Hand'.

The lyrics, in retrospect, were utterly heartbreaking.

Chapter 51

Great Expectations

That initial taste of freedom was exceptional.

I felt like a kid in a sweet shop: no alarm, no timetable, hours spent walking on the beach, stretching out my entire body, thinking and breathing in the sea air as if my life depended on it, sleeping in as my brain and body caught up with each other, and the tension and anxiety I had been holding onto for months, easing out of me. I wasn't proud of having dropped out of school mid-term, but every part of me had told me I had to change something, and I instinctively knew it was the right choice.

The place we were staying in was more suited as a summer rental. It was cramped, chilly and damp in places, but I didn't care. Waking up in the morning and being able to go back to sleep felt like such a treat, each moment a feeling of freedom, and although I was still heavy with grief, my main feeling was that I had made the right move.

He didn't.

One morning feeling invigorated after days of proper rest and fresh air, I squeezed myself alongside him as he showered in the narrow cubicle. He shoved me away, looking at me as if I was off my tree, asking what the hell was wrong with me. Seeing my humiliated and red face, he covered his irritation, laughing: '*Amor, there is very little room in here for one person! Not even enough water for two, and I have to go to work.'* He hadn't been fast enough, his disgust clear to see. Mortified and turning away, I agreed it had been a silly idea. With tears stinging my eyes, the hard reality was I had become revolting to my husband.

Finding ways of uniting us was futile but I suggested swimming in the sea: cold, fun and free. I loved it because, for a few minutes, swimming under the icy water, I forgot to hate myself and felt deliciously new again. He joined me and handed me his phone to capture the moment for his social media. *'Take loads,'* he commanded, *'that way, at least one will come out because you are crap at taking photos.'* Things were breaking down between us at a rate I couldn't quite believe. Spending most of the time at work fifty minutes down the road, he preferred to remain there overnight. According to him, it wasn't worth the cost of fuel to come back and drive in again the following morning, and he was vague about where he was staying.

Communication was restricted to long, detailed messages from me, attempting to explain my feelings. If he replied, it was short and terse. His long silences made me feel anxious as if my showing up to live with him again was unwanted and could have been avoided if only I had kept my side of the bargain and stayed put, although he never actually said that.

> **SILENT TREATMENT**
> YET ANOTHER FORM OF CONTROL TO CREATE WORRY AND TENSION, A USEFUL FORM OF PUNISHMENT SHOULD YOU CAUSE UPSET OR DENT THEIR EGO, ALSO A GREAT AVOIDANCE TACTIC WHILE SIMULTANEOUSLY CRUSHING YOUR SELF-ESTEEM. A CHILLING WIN-WIN.

To justify my presence, I overcompensated – I may as well have stood in a line with my hand up pleading, *'pick me, pick me'* - spending time preparing tasty meals, buying decent wine, working hard at making the dank apartment cosy and homely while spending time and money managing the refurb on the beach house. To prove my earning worth, I was also busy with extra online lessons, pretending to everyone I was having the time of my life and hadn't swapped one nightmare for another.

Christmas came and went in a series of arguments and wrong presents and his ill-concealed boredom at having to spend time with me. He bought me cheap, short, clinging, unsuitable dresses and expressed annoyance at my ingratitude: *'It's your favourite shop, isn't it?'* My carefully thought out and often expensive presents to him were ruthlessly discarded with a wry smile. *'You can send them back, right?'* he asked, as if that was the point, but caring even less. I had been generous and done my best, but it wasn't right; his Christmas ruined by my misery and bad moods.

A rollercoaster of accusations and hugs, vitriol followed by soft, cajoling, verbal affection, left me feeling as if I was walking in a maze of mirrors, distorted and twisted as I was turned every which way. Everything was tied to his needs, wants and happiness, making my own irrelevant. Unsuccessful in whatever efforts I made to be the person he expected, although I was no longer sure of who that was or where to find her, and feeling my throat constrict at my attempts to speak, I tried to defend myself: *'My dad-'* I stammered, but I was cut short:

'Everyone's parents die, stop using him as an excuse for what you are.' I raised my hands in fury and he caught my wrists as I tried to lash out against him while his grinning, victorious reaction proved what a monster I had become.

Chapter 52

It ain't what you do

It was early 2021. I had lost my Dad less than six months before, and now I was fast losing myself.

Like a wrecking ball, along came another lockdown. With no real reason to disappear, he had more mood swings than a pre-menstrual teenager: euphoric one moment and frighteningly down the next, finding fault with everything related to the renovation. Now, instead of working, he spent long hours smoking, chatting, and advising the builder.

Infuriated at how much longer everything was taking because of these chats, I was accused of excluding him from the project because of my love of 'controlling'. Returning from long walks to try and avoid the rows, he'd pull me towards him, explaining how he was only looking out for me and the money I was spending, that he had gone down there to check on the work because the builder was drinking too much or was lazy, but his own efforts to be helpful were clearly not valued as I was so unwilling to let him have a say. It sounded so plausible. He could obviously see things I couldn't, coloured by my desperate need to be liked by the people I saw every day. I needed to be more savvy, more aware. *'You are too kind,'* he told me, *'you need to be careful.'* I felt both foolish and relieved.

PROJECTION
'IT WASN'T ME!' THIS ONE IS A CHILDLIKE DEFENCE TACTIC USED TO PIVOT THE BLAME OF THEIR ACTIONS ONTO OTHERS WHILE SIMULTANEOUSLY CLAIMING ALTRUISM. DOUBLE WHAMMY: I'M DOING THIS FOR YOU, AND YOU DON'T APPRECIATE ME. OFTEN DISGUISED AS AN ACCUSATION, MORE OFTEN THAN NOT, COVERING THEIR OWN CULPABILITY. TRY TURNING THEIR WORDS AROUND BECAUSE WHATEVER YOU ARE BEING ACCUSED OF IS EXACTLY WHAT THEY THEMSELVES ARE DOING, THINKING OR FEELING. GUARANTEED.

His anxieties were endless: upsetting the neighbour, no work, managing the dog, one insurmountable wall after another, to the point where I became seriously worried he could be depressed. I made a conscious effort to cheer him up during walks on the beach, building him up with excited nuggets of progress and plans of how it would all work out.

Positivity was unwelcome, and my optimism met with snarky, contemptuous put-downs about my ignorance and understanding of how things worked. One day, I'd had enough and exploded. Sick and tired of being unable to penetrate this negative and antagonistic barrier of gloom, retaliating angrily, I asked why he was always complaining, putting up obstacles and creating issues. *'Why is everything such a problem for you? Why, when I am doing my best, are you so damned miserable?'* I shouted, my frustrated resentment coming through loud and clear. Satisfied his mood had resulted in the evaporation of my happiness and the appearance of my tearful temper, he looked at me, pausing, then scathingly, he said:

'Well, look at you... hardly surprising your ex-husband left you.'

Standing on that cold, windy beach, hearing those words leaving the lips that so easily uttered the words *I love you*, I looked at his face, thinking maybe I had misheard: it was too cruel to honestly believe it. I stammered out a reply: *'You know why. The IVF... he was cheating.'* He looked at me, his eyes narrowing, *'Yeah, maybe, but he must have had good reason...'* Shrugging, he turned to shield the roll-up he was lighting from the elements.

Tears streaming down my face, I had no comeback because, this time, he had rendered me speechless. I walked away; my insides leaden. Much later, he found me pale-faced with swollen eyes, curled up in a ball on the sofa, pretending to concentrate on something else. Sensing perhaps he had gone too far but unwilling to accept any responsibility, he brushed off the severity of the pain his words may have caused. *'We always say things to hurt in an argument, it doesn't actually mean anything.'*

I was meaningless.

My physical response was to start shrinking and retreating into myself, trying to hide the person I had become, not wishing to inflict myself on anyone. Going out anywhere, he acted bullishly and arrogant, always striding slightly ahead as if disassociating himself from me, or maybe I hung back for the very same reasons. In rare conversations with others we met, he answered quickly for me, highlighting my *'Englishness'*, revelling in my discomfort at their stares and then smiling softly at me for everyone to see who was the good guy, my frowning, pained expression dark and sad compared to his grinning, sunny affable disposition.

I had become a shrew-like, complaining nag obsessed only with insignificant issues. *'Are we still talking about THAT?'* he'd ask in disbelief, and I was dizzy and confused as to why my questions were seriously bothering him, whatever they were or however they were asked. Why did I always have to go on and on? Couldn't I forget the small stuff stifling us both so much? Orange juice spilled carelessly and left to go sticky, clothes abandoned, doors, cupboards and drawers slammed or left wide open.

'Why. Can't. You. Just. Let. It. Go?' His question to everything I asked, reminded or requested of him. Ironically, for years I had indeed let everything go, barely question-

ing, never probing, trusting and believing whatever he said. Now I was being blamed for the miserable minutiae in our lives, and the absent, carefree, fun-loving person I once was had now (according to him) been replaced by a chore-obsessed, moody, unhappy bitch.

Was there anything left worth fighting for? I could imagine my dad frowning his disapproval at my readiness to give up on my marriage. Then where would I go? Who would want me? Trapped in a lockdown, trying to hide and remain inconspicuous while evidently not being invisible enough was driving me nuts. Nothing I did or said made either one of us happy, so naturally, I looked for an alternative to break that cycle, not break *us*, but interrupt our despair and find a solution.

I suggested separation, cushioning the jarring word with the acceptance that no one was to blame; it happened sometimes, and we could try to amicably move forward with a view to a brighter and happier future. I didn't suggest it lightly, either, wanting us to talk it through and discuss the best way forward. Separation was the last thing I wanted, but sometimes, such a final word is needed as a wake-up call.

I may as well have asked him to move the car.

'*If that is what you want, OK,*' he responded. '*We always do what you want, anyway.*' Adding a postscript note of venom, he said, '*This is no doubt because you have money coming to you, so you will be fine.*' Considering I had spent the best part of the last decade supporting two of us with as many jobs as I could fit in, this was a low blow. Money: damned if I had it, damned if I didn't. The stinging shot of culpability hurt but, connected as it was to my dad, something deep inside me reared up and told him to piss off and take the biggest drink of fuck off he could find. Spitting the words out in a fury I was unaware I was still capable of, I furiously spelled it out for him :

*It **certainly** wasn't **always** my fault or what **I** wanted, and **I** hadn't instigated the possibility of separation because he had spilt some orange juice or hadn't bothered to make the bed. **I*** *wanted a life more than anything with the man I had married, but if it was a never-ending, one-sided road of perpetual misery and insults, then I had nothing left to give, and he, for his part, had demonstrably given nothing at all.*

As if anticipating this very reaction, he stepped forward as if to remove me from the precipice I was edging towards, and his eyes grew large with hurt while his loving arms and shy smile reeled me back in, whispering words of comfort and reassurance. He was just terribly worried, he told me, while not actually addressing a single point I had mentioned. It wasn't a question of rooting out the cause of our disintegrating relationship; the idea of us breaking up was out of the question and something he had no intention of entertaining, so he ignored it and instead gave me, his primary supply, morsels of affection to maintain that tenuous bond.

> **SUPPLY**
> THAT WAS WHAT I WAS. WHEN YOU RENOUNCE YOUR OWN NEEDS TO MAINTAIN THEIRS. MATERIAL? EMOTIONAL? WHATEVER YOU HAVE BECOMES THEIRS, AND THE MORE YOU GIVE, THE LESS YOU BECOME, UNTIL YOU ARE NOTHING. HOWEVER, DON'T EXPECT THEM TO WALK AWAY UNTIL THE NEW SUPPLY IS READY. WALKING AWAY TAKES COURAGE AND BACK-BONE, AND THEY'D RATHER HAVE YOU ON A LEASH.

Well aware that, while waiting for probate to conclude, I had also been seriously considering buying a small investment flat in my home city, tentatively, he broached the alternative idea of using the money to buy a larger place in Italy for us *with* a garden for the dog. Such a wise investment, he enthused, so much more available for your money, encouragingly listing the numerous advantages. I had never considered buying in Italy, but listening to his reasoning, I realised that it made more sense, and I agreed to look at potential properties.

All talk of separation disappeared along with my idea of a place for me in England. With plenty of free time, as his job was still on hold and a new mission to sink his sharp teeth into, he started searching for the ideal place. In many respects, this new plan brought us briefly closer as we discussed stories of incompetent estate agents and missed appointments. We giggled in astonishment at the deluded greedy minds of sellers whose dilapidated, overpriced properties required far more than a 'touch of modernisation'.

I was in England when a potential property was found through the builder's neighbours. *'Fantastic people,'* he gushed down the phone. *'You'd love them. Well, her, anyway, she is so funny, great company whereas he is much older, but her, well, she's exactly our type of person.'* I no longer knew what our type of person was, but the house was indeed love at first sight when I set eyes on it. The garden was a huge overgrown jungle, and the untouched inside was desperate for an overhaul. It was solid and structurally sound but in desperate need of love and attention. He was all over the new property as if he was investing his own money, planning our future, motivated and excited; it felt infectious. I had been too quick to consider separation. This was our very own home, a dream about to happen. I held on to those pockets of positive moments, believing them to be proof of a marriage worth saving, of two people destined to be together, at the same time, pushing to the back of my mind the inexplicable sickening feeling I had when we were together.

Taking me somewhere new for my birthday, high up on a cliff, we walked down towards a cove, passing close to the edge and watching the waves crash beneath us against the jagged rocks. He egged me on to jump in: *'Go on,'* he encouraged, *'it's not that high and you can swim. You always claim you like a challenge,'* he mocked. Looking down at the 30 m sheer drop, frowning, trying to work out if he was joking, I walked on saying nothing. The rest of the day was spent enjoying the sun and a pizza picnic, and his surprise bottle of chilled white wine was a surprising and unexpected touch. All in all, it was a fairly pleasant day marred only by his clumsy attempts to have sex with me on a public beach.

From offering tiny pieces of emotional sustenance to withholding any and all emotion, I continued to teeter on this tightrope he pulled and loosened at will—a sick game of minor indulgence or major deprivation while I constantly picked up crumbs of anything good in our lives, believing in a return to how we were. Each time, the hugs to bring me back onside were fleeting, cursory and never quite truly heartfelt, the promises a little more vague, a lot less flowery, leading me to believe I might well have a regenerative heart condition. My eternally optimistic heart waited patiently for a caring look or a kind word, and when it came, blood rushed through its very core, filling it up with love, anticipating more of the same.

TRAUMA BONDING
THE HOLY GRAIL OF NARCISSISM. MONTHS, YEARS, AND DECADES SPENT ENSURING YOU ARE EMOTIONALLY WELDED TO THEM NOW MANIFEST INTO PULLING YOUR STRINGS IN EVERY DIRECTION; YOUR CONSTANT OVERRIDING BELIEF IS THIS 'DECENT' PERSON TO WHOM YOU OWE A DEBT OF GRATITUDE AND LOVE EVEN THOUGH THEIR BEHAVIOUR SAYS THE OPPOSITE. MEANWHILE, THEY LOOK ON IN SEMI-CREDULOUS LOATHING AT YOUR CAPACITY TO LOVE WHILE TREATING YOU AS VIRTUALLY WORTHLESS.

One beautiful spring morning at the beach house, I heard an unfamiliar car pulling up outside. Watching as he sauntered towards it and leaned right into the passenger window, not quite blocking out the woman in the driver's seat, I had a visceral physical reaction. My legs started to shake, and I felt my stomach drop in panic. I saw him indicate towards the property, and I made myself walk outside. They briefly glanced at me, and she accelerated quickly, driving off. He stepped back in wordlessly, not looking in my direction, forcing me to ask, *'Who was that?'*

Without missing a beat, he replied, *'So and so, I told you, her and her boyfriend were interested in renting this place, they wanted it for a long-term rent, but I told them it was booked up.*

Surely, you remember me telling you?' He walked back inside, barely looking at me.

PATHOLOGICAL LYING
WRAPPED IN FLUFFY UNNECESSARY DETAILS AND WITH A SPOONFUL OF A SNEERING TONE THAT YOU HAVE ONCE AGAIN 'FORGOTTEN' THEY TOLD YOU ALREADY. LYING COMES AS NATURALLY AND EASILY TO A NARCISSIST AS BREATHING.

Liar, liar pants on fire.

Chapter 53

That's Not My Name

Still hopeful, excited and optimistic because our lives (on paper) looked pretty damn good: we had a great business in the now beautifully renovated beach place property, our own house to sort, and, with lockdown ending, he would soon have his job. Surely, despite the worst few years of our lives, things were going to be OK.

We were fighting for our marriage, and to demonstrate how united we were, I planned on us going into Rome for his birthday. I knew how much he missed the city; a lovely lunch in his favourite restaurant and some shopping together would be ideal. Initially reticent, he begged me not to invite anyone else, not even as a surprise. This from the man who loved big celebrations with him playing the protagonist, so clocking my surprise, he added as a sweetener: '*I just want it to be us.*' I was pleased, but later, he casually mentioned two other friends who would be joining us. Well, it was his birthday, after all.

Over lunch, the girl shyly handed him some Ralph Lauren cashmere gloves, which he accepted, squeezing her hand and smiled. '*Finally! Someone who really knows me.*' I couldn't help but think how wonderful it was, him being spoilt by others, and how kind he had been, considering he hated gloves. In the glow of his delighted expression, she positively beamed, and they quickly excused themselves to nip outside for a quick cigarette while his other friend kept me busy asking endless questions about renovations.

* * *

While waiting for the house contracts, the owners gave me free rein to start on the garden, so I happily grew an abundance of tomatoes, cucumbers, peppers and aubergines. Never having attempted to grow anything more than a pot of basil, I loved the feel of the earth and seeing the shoots coming through; they seemed to me the only thing I was able to make a difference to, and I loved them even more for it.

Watching me cultivate and toil the earth and chat away to my plants, he laughingly referred to me as a '*Contadina*' (peasant). It wasn't affectionate, more of a veiled insult, which I ignored, along with the many things he called me to avoid using my actual name. Forrest Gump was another because I often walked on my own for miles. Seeing my face fall at this new moniker, he groaned at my sensitivity: '*You used to have a sense of humour,*' he complained. In front of others, he used '*Amo*', a lazy, slang-style abbreviation meant to denote '*amore*' or 'luv'. A really ugly one was '*Aaaaooohhh*'; even on the phone he answered with this anonymous and vulgar Roman slang, underlining my faceless presence in his world.

Less than keen on the back-breaking work involved in managing the overgrown garden, he preferred the beach, which he felt was '*the whole point*' of living by the sea, so he left me to it, disappearing for hours on end. When possible, he also sloped off to the capital on '*work errands*' for his future boss, telling me, at the last minute, that he needed to stay overnight. I had no idea where he slept because any time I asked for details, the stories changed, interwoven with intricate excuses and elaborate tales backed up by 'friends' I no longer spoke to.

I tried to care where he was, but I didn't, as his absences were easier to deal with than his company. When he did show up, he liked to shake the very foundations of my newfound peace by picking fights near the open windows of my new home. Shouting and screaming just like in the old days, only this time every nasty word could be heard and understood. I wasn't having my tranquillity threatened, *not here*, after I had worked so hard to create a sane and safe place away from the aggression I was regularly coming across in my marriage. Quietly refusing to rise to his taunts, defiantly closing the windows or walking away to another room far from the cursing and foul language, he liked to shout for the benefit of my new neighbours—something he avoided at his place.

Often resentful, he repeatedly asked why we couldn't stay at the finished beach house and disagreed with renting it out. '*Why can't we enjoy it now that it's done?*' he moaned. I patiently explained the need to build up the business as neither of us were working, suggesting 'camping' at the house as fun, especially as it was now hot enough to take cold showers. My cajolery fell on offended and entitled ears, and despite bargaining with him as you might a toddler enticing him with BBQs and tasty vegetable concoctions, roughing it was not for him; he wanted to go into town alone to eat 'properly' at a restaurant or to his friend's bar. Meanwhile, I prepared homegrown salads, bought mozzarella and made the dusty terrace look pretty with candles and a table set up for one.

Being alone was not only all too familiar but was becoming preferable.

Arranging for us to go out for the day with friends who owned an RIB, he insisted I took a load of homegrown veg with me as well as wine and sandwiches for the picnic. Doubting this would be welcome, he assured me the vegetables would be perfect.

Making all the right noises when I handed over a bunch of multi-coloured aubergines, peppers and tomatoes to virtual strangers, I felt more than slightly embarrassed as they tried to find room on the small boat to store them, the profound feeling of awkward discomfort stirred up memories of scone-making in Rome nearly thirty years previously. Loud laughter carried through the air as he talked about his English 'peasant' wife and her allotment accomplishments while I sat miserably humiliated at the back wishing I was anywhere else. But most of all, wishing I hadn't brought groceries.

Setting off, I willed myself not to cry. The lump in my throat was as big as a golf ball, but I needn't have worried; no one was paying me any attention.

The archipelago was stunning. You couldn't help but be impressed and overawed by the sheer beauty. Mooring the boat in the gorgeous clear waters, four of us swam out to a grotto, where I was told we needed to swim through an underwater cave to reach the other part. I decided I would refuse as this ticked every nightmare box I had. When we arrived, shouting encouragement, they all reassured me it was only a short distance, so not wanting to disappoint, I reluctantly went underneath with him swimming right behind me. A few seconds under, and I predictably panicked as the space narrowed. Unable to see ahead and turning slightly, I gestured my fear to his masked face. He stared impassively at me and blocked my exit; he didn't move. With no choice but to go forward, I turned and swam, coming up the other side with my heart banging, feeling scared and out of breath but relieved to be through. Nodding to the couple, I indicated I would swim the longer way round in the open sea rather than go under again.

He didn't offer to come with me or check I was okay; he didn't even swim behind me to make sure I arrived back safely; instead, he swam back through the grotto with his mates. The sea current was strong, but I kept going until I reached the boat, and seeing me approach, he swam towards me, shouting in English, '*I am so, so proud of my wife, well done!*' I was completely confused, something felt really wrong, really off, but I didn't know what.

'*Why didn't you let me turn back?*' I asked, frowning.

'*So proud of you,*' he repeated loudly for everyone, ignoring my question, as I climbed, shaking and tired, back into the boat.

There was something truly bloody-minded and stubborn about the how I constantly clung to the relationship—if I just did *this*, said *that*, bought *the other*. The irony was the more I tried to showcase my ability to be the best wife I could, the more he despised me. My discard was well underway; I just wasn't aware of it.

DISCARD
NO LONGER OF ANY REAL USE TO THEM, YOU TRY EVERYTHING POSSIBLE IN YOUR NOW TINY WORLD TO MAKE THEM SEE YOU. THE ABUSE IS NOW IN FULL THROTTLE, AND WHETHER YOU ARE HUMILIATED, IGNORED OR ULTIMATELY WALKED OUT ON, THE WHOLE POINT OF THIS VICIOUS PERIOD IS TO MAKE YOU FEEL AS WORTHLESS AS POSSIBLE.

We were invited for lunch to discuss the sale of the house, and reaching the end of the meal, we were joined by another couple. I watched the girl as she extended her hand out for a piece of the cheese he was cutting. *'Hard or soft?'* he asked her. She smiled seductively at him, *'Hard, obviously,'* she said, *'I like it hard.'* Later, at home, I asked him about that comment. Pretending to look baffled, he lied, *'I didn't hear that, are you sure she said it?'* His eyes wide in innocence, and bulging too with guilt. Seeing my sceptical expression, he started laughing and joked, *'As if I'd ever go near that.'*

The end of that utterly miserable summer took him back to Rome and his job cleaning the rooms in the boutique B&B his friend owned. With the advent of his independence and freedom, I prayed for an ending to his vile moods; instead, he veered between euphoria and frustration, which for once wasn't directed at me but at the excessive and allegedly uncontrollable drinking habits and stammering rants of his friend/boss/business partner (the title of whom depended on his audience). If he called, he lifted his phone so I could hear the madman ranting in the passenger seat next to him. *'See what I have to put up with?'* he said as I expressed my disbelief.

I picked him up from the train station one day. I wore a gorgeous dress, tanned, slim and excited, ready to sign the final documents for the house. Grinning, I hugged him, and climbing into the car, he stared at me as if *seeing* me for the first time: '*Wow,*' he said, '*I'd forgotten how beautiful you are.*'

It wasn't a compliment; it was a *comparison*.

Chapter 54

Suddenly I See

The colour of those last four months from September to December 2021 changed from the subtle black, white and grey tones of the previous decade to an angry blood red, thickly splattered across any time we spent together. Weekends were merely a countdown of time with him meticulously washing and preparing clothes and himself for his upcoming week.

Often borrowing my car to go to work, he had started dropping heavy hints about how much he needed his own, especially as he was now suffering back trouble from using mine. Occasionally taking the train in, he found this mortifying because, at his age, he felt a man *needed* his own transport. Aside from his general distaste for public transport, his freedom was seriously curtailed, as the choice to come home was infuriatingly not his. With neither the means nor the inclination to buy himself a car, he set to work on me.

Unexpectedly, I was not the financial pushover he had anticipated. As far as I was concerned, running two cars for two people was an unnecessary expense I was unwilling to fork out for; plus, the trains were both efficient and cost-effective and a ten-minute walk from his job, so I told him he was lucky to have two options. Whining, he said it wasn't fair on me having to drive to the station, but this time, I was ready: '*Not a problem,*' I said, '*it only takes five minutes.*' Finding me harder than usual to bend over backwards for him, he tried using safety as a reason: *'I don't like you being here without transport, if anything happens to you or Buddy, you need a car.'*

Not a husband... a car.

Suspecting a downturn in my hitherto endless generosity and needing transport autonomy he switched tactics; a bigger car would give him the freedom to return midweek to see *'his family'* creating a joyful work/life balance! What's more we could use the extra time to take the dog for walks in the woods, something I longed for as I knew how much Buddy relished walking in that pine forest but was nervous of going alone in my Mini. With that persuasive method and those completely fake assurances – the promise of the three of us all riding around in a bigger car, going to more places, doing different things – he forced the altogether stronger me back down in the dark preventing her from speaking up because in that moment his words held the power.

> **BREADCRUMBING**
> TINY MORSELS OF HOPE THROWN INTERMITTENTLY IN YOUR DIRECTION OUTLINING THE VERY THING YOU WANT OR NEED, PROMISING IT CONVINCINGLY WITH THE EMPTIEST OF WORDS SO YOU CAN THEN BE MANIPULATED INTO FULFILLING THEIR IMMEDIATE DESIRE, USING A SUBJECT OR PERSON CLOSE TO YOU TO BREAK YOU DOWN AND AGREE. ONLY TO LATER REJECT ANY CLAIMS THAT HAD BEEN THEIR INTENTION.

Yet again, I believed it all, and lent him the money for that mid-life crisis jeep, He returned home less frequently than before, while 'our' dog wasn't allowed anywhere near it.

My life was now split: alone with Buddy, living back in the beach house as the season had ended, and now, overseeing the new house renovations and teaching online. All this and coping with stomach-churning anxiety as I waited vainly for messages alerting me of his possible return but also dreading it because it was just horrible, from the moment he arrived, no longer hiding how much he didn't want to be there.

On one memorable occasion, he returned bullish and arrogant. Attacking me, he raised the issue of no intimacy: '*How do you think it makes me feel that my wife has a vibrator?*' he asked smugly as if this was the perfect line to stop me in my tracks. Looking up at this man who didn't have an independent thought in his head, I retorted, '*How do YOU think it made me feel having to buy one?*' Speechless, he stood there open-mouthed; evidently, whoever had provided him with his 'killer' line hadn't given him a follow-up.

Conversational enquiries about his week in the capital or his job were scornfully rejected as I couldn't possibly understand: from the appalling traffic to impossible parking, from his '*idiot*' alcoholic boss to spiralling fuel costs and general work fatigue, I knew nothing at all, living as I did a sheltered and charmed life by the beach.

Listening to his baseless accusations, having carried a great deal myself for the previous decade, I did answer back, but unwilling to hear any logical and therefore unwanted reasoning, his vile response of '*Stop barking at me*' was screamed in my face as he covered his ears doing a fine job of impersonating a tall, hysterical toddler. A barrage of fiery, nasty outbursts ensued, culminating in him packing up his car and driving off with the excuse he needed to leave me yet again to my misery.

My stomach clenched as, once again, I started the week picking up the fragmented pieces, trying to put myself back together.

Buying groceries and filling up the fridge, the stronger girl inside me quietly insisted I take little pinches of control back; no more of the sparkling water he preferred nor the bottle of rum he liked as an after-dinner drink. The Tabasco, too, he happily poured all over the dishes I cooked ran out and wasn't replaced. The large chunks of expensive parmesan, the cured sausages, spicy salami, salty pecorino, all those little extras he had taken for granted for so long, gradually disappeared.

Spiteful little gestures of non-compliance made me feel guilty but slyly happy.

He never spent a penny on me, never bought a plant for the new place or created a drawing, not a single item to even pretend I had occurred to him while he was away. Mentioning this once had resulted in his turning up the following week and carelessly throwing a bunch of cheap carnations on the worktop, watching me closely, waiting to pounce if I expressed anything other than delight and appreciation.

One Saturday, suggesting lunch out somewhere, he looked delighted. When I innocently asked if he would be paying, I watched in amused disbelief as he looked momentarily distraught and actually *physically* tapped his pockets, saying, *'Oh no, I put my wages in the safe at work and completely forgot to bring them.'* It was a ludicrously far-fetched lie, but I was fast learning that interrogation was pointless, knowing already his response: *'Why would I make up something like that? Who do you think I am?'*

He fed me so many lies I was choking on them, unable to keep track of which toxic seeds he had been sowing and to whom. If confronted by the truth, he resorted to flat-out denial. *'I didn't say that, they misunderstood'* became his mantra, laying the blame firmly on whoever wasn't present and therefore unable to defend themselves. His tendency to exaggeration had always been considered a joke, but now I could see it hid a lifetime of stinking, festering, invented crap; the reality was sickening because I'd been busy spiralling into virtual madness trying to work out if I had misunderstood, misheard or even imagined things he had said, when all along, the simple, ironic truth is, when you trust someone implicitly, you have handed them their very own *Get Out Of Jail Free card*.

His malice, beautifully masked in a cloak of feigned innocence, proved tricky to identify, but I was slowly waking up to the very real correlation between his presence and my pitiful lack of self-esteem.

Remarkably, by abandoning me to my own devices and with no one else to turn to, I sought out the only one who could actually help answer my questions: myself. The long-forgotten feisty creature I used to be, and now needed more than ever, was not only there fighting to be heard, but she was also royally pissed off. Long walks by the sea spent evaluating, dissecting and assessing every single discussion, row and hateful word exchanged energized the person I used to be, and I could hear her answer becoming louder and louder.

'It's not me, it's not me, IT'S NOT ME.'

Chapter 55

Unmasked

Sticks and Stones May Break My Bones – blah blah blah bullshit.

Words, insults, and slow insidious degradation built up over years don't just hurt; they cause a network of doubt and pain, seeping and bleeding and becoming such an intrinsic part of your character that they influence your behaviour, responses and reactions.

A lifetime of subtle put-downs, 'amusing' slights, jibes, snubs and barbs chased quickly with the weak caveat '*I was only joking, whatever's the matter with you?*' meant my own boundaries were non-existent. So preoccupied that I might be misconstrued, excluded or cause offence, I allowed myself to be OK with how I was spoken to. Snappy, curt words belie the deep damage they cause, creating within you a sense that you *should* be OK accepting harsh words instead of speaking up. Covering that hurt for a long time with sarcasm, dark humour, or occasionally biting back with the very spikiness I was so often accused of.

Like the machine at the airport wrapping protective plastic around baggage, round and round, making identification impossible, I felt I was also covered up in layer upon layer of what was permissible, allowed, things I was and wasn't supposed to say or do, see or hear. Initially soft and gentle, advising and recommending, but over time, becoming tighter, more constricting, binding me, holding me down and silencing me.

I'd had enough and was now properly fighting my way out of that suffocating film, clawing and pushing against everything that was so entrenched that it had prevented who I really was from surfacing.

There wasn't much I could actually do *to* him as I didn't truly grasp what was going on aside from the fact we didn't make each other happy; on the other hand, I did know that there was plenty I could do to protect myself. I stopped engaging, saying only the bare minimum, avoiding him and, therefore, the rows. Reminiscent of my hiding in the bathroom, only this time, I wasn't hysterical and lashing out; I was quiet and detached, infuriating him as it didn't tie in with his preferred label of me as the insane hot-headed savage he had the misfortune to be married to, and try as he might, to keep a hold of the reins they were loosening.

His attempts to control me were ongoing and masked in the 'innocence' I now found nauseatingly transparent. Leaving to go for a walk with the dog, he pocketed both sets of keys, making sure I was unable to leave while he was out. It worked beautifully as I spent a frantic hour searching, and when he eventually appeared, he pulled out my set from his pocket, gasping in feigned surprise. Registering my irritation, he gave me a half-smile, and in a sing-song voice, he said, 'Sorreeee.' But I wasn't won over. '*Oh my god,*' he said, dismissing my concerns, '*it isn't like I took them on* purpose, *it was a mistake!*'

Wiser now to his nastiness and unpredictability, knowing he would do anything to ruin the only few hours I had to myself before he drove back to Rome, I understood my need to be one step ahead. Without divulging my plans for the morning, after all, I had no idea where he was most of the week, and waiting to hear the click of the gate with my heart racing in case he returned unexpectedly, I grabbed everything I needed and left, quickly walking up to the one place I felt entirely at ease.

My home.

I had already stopped taking him to the new house, a subconscious move made by the stronger part of me. The moment I walked in that front door, I relaxed, enjoying the peaceful solitude of caring for the new baby plants, changing their pots and soil, watering and mooching around amongst the dust and debris of the building site while listening to *The Archers* omnibus, a peaceful connection to my dad—my idea of heaven.

Unfortunately, I underestimated his wish to create chaos in my life.

On one such Sunday morning, quietly pottering contentedly in dirty clothes, appreciating the tranquillity, my phone rang.

'I have no keys,' he said grumpily. *'You need to come back now and open up.* Instantly annoyed, I asked why he had no keys, my exasperation clear. *'I didn't think I needed them, how the hell was I to know you were going out?'* he said, furious that I was questioning him. I was about to say you never go anywhere without them, but interrupting me in a tone matching my own, he said, *'I am here with Buddy, who desperately needs to eat, are we really doing this now?'*

I was raging, but mostly with myself for not anticipating his underhand, predictable actions. Locking up my place and driving back down, I wordlessly opened the gate and the front door. Turning to leave, I asked in a normal voice if he could please, *please* remember to always take his keys. He hadn't finished with me yet: *'You could have just waited, and then none of this would have happened, but no, you have to do what YOU want, making EVERYONE wait for you.'*

'For fuck's sake,' I responded angrily under my breath. Not wanting to add anything else, I turned to walk away.

'That's right,' he taunted, *'walk away, as usual. That's what you do when you don't like what is being said, when you KNOW it's the truth.'*

Breathing deeply, I left, thinking to myself: *Don't say a word, not a word, do not engage, walk away, walk away.*

Back at mine, feeling badly affected by the events of the morning, talking to myself and questioning why and how, every so often, I'd be caught out. I felt a sob in my throat, and hot, angry tears appeared as I went over all the details. Absorbed in my planting and rumination, I was really startled when he unexpectedly appeared at the door, all dressed up and entirely nonplussed by that morning's disagreement. Smiling pleasantly, he said, *'Shall we go out for lunch then?'*

Shocked to see him and even more alarmed to hear him speaking as if this had all been agreed in advance, I actually staggered back a few steps as he stood in the doorway and stared at him, momentarily speechless. *'What's the matter?'* he asked as if I had forgotten our lunch date. *'Can't we just go and have a nice lunch somewhere, you know, do something normal?'* he sighed.

I walked towards him and, barely speaking above an incredulous whisper, I indicated with my hand from his head to his feet: *'Did I do this?'* I asked. *'Have you always been this way? Or is it because of something I did to create…* THIS?' For just a few seconds, the benign, pleasant expression slipped, his eyes blackened, and a cold, angry, menacing look took hold.

I looked at him, and before turning away, I said quietly, *'I have no idea who you are.'*

Chapter 56

Nearly There

Believing a separation was inevitable, I cancelled his ticket for our holiday back to England in December; it was unthinkable to pretend we were united in front of my friends and family at Christmas.

Appalled at my bold and decisive move to go alone and leave him behind was further proof he wasn't listening to me. After a week in Rome, he returned with a far more positive slant. *'Yes, I agree, I think this is exactly what you need, some time away with your family and friends, a break, it will do you good.'*

As if I was the nut-job who needed a retreat, and he was magnanimously allowing it.

Any serious discussions regarding the process for a separation were either ignored or dismissed as preposterous. I learned how to initiate it at the local town hall offices and painstakingly explained it to his blank face. Trying to elicit some sort of response, I asked if he was in agreement. He bitterly dismissed his own input as irrelevant because *'this is all your decision, and you always do what you want'*. Sitting down opposite him and genuinely curious, I calmly asked him, *'If you were married to you, would you stay?'* With dull predictability, he replied, *'I've tried everything, but nothing I do is ever good enough for you.'*

'*Okay,*' I continued slowly, '*please, please tell me what exactly you have done?*' It wasn't a test; I was simply trying to see if I could penetrate this wall of banality. '*I understand you think you have done your best, me too, yet here we are. Please tell me one single thing you have brought to the table to save our marriage.*'

He looked around him, embarrassed. Unable to answer or look me in the face, he eventually mumbled something pathetically. Apparently, '*Doing everything he could*' meant he had a cleaning job.

The absurd reality was I truly hoped he might finally understand what he was about to lose. Divorce had never been mentioned for this very reason because a teeny tiny part of me believed this could all be pulled back, saved by some heroic effort, but one that would have to come from him. As far as I was concerned, I couldn't and *wouldn't* do any more, unaware that my refusal to cater to his every whim was the real death knell of this relationship.

The rosy optimism that there was anything decent in him was to take yet another battering when, unabashed, he lied directly to my face, and I could no longer deny who he was.

It was the start of December, and once again, he was pleading poverty: '*I have no money this month,*' he wailed. '*I have to pay my car insurance, and then there is the monthly payment to you for the car.*'

'*No, you don't,*' I said, my eyes fixed on his face. '*Your 82-year-old father has paid for your car insurance, according to the bank transfer.*'

Momentarily blindsided, his mouth fell open, his black eyes popping out of his skull in a familiar guilty reflex. The humiliation as he realised he'd been caught was brief and quickly covered by garbled lies, justification and a stammered denial. I watched in silence, listening as he tied himself further up in knots. There you are, I thought, feeling repelled and fascinated. '*It's not what you think,*' he pleaded, but I had nothing left to say.

* * *

On New Year's Eve in 2021, alone in my Airbnb, I felt a large lump under my armpit.

Sitting bolt upright in bed, barely able to think straight, panicking, I moved my hand across it, pushing and feeling: *it couldn't be back, it mustn't be back, I couldn't go through all that again.* Touching the area and the skin around it, I could see the last few years of stress, pain, loneliness and grief flash before me, leading to the return of the one thing I had barely been able to cope with the first time around. I wondered if this was what drowning people meant when they described seeing their lives in a series of images as they lost consciousness.

Only, I was drowning in thoughts.

Examining the lump in the mirror and catching sight of my pale, tear-stained face, it hit me harder than a punch in the face that I was entirely on my own. Telling him about this would mean him grabbing onto it in the same way he had when my dad had died, an excuse to play the hero to insignificant people whose validation he worshipped. His interest would be purely selfish, an opportunity to demonstrate how he always stepped up in the face of tragedy to anyone who happened to glance at his social media status.

My mind reluctantly slipped back to the first time, his one dreadful attendance at chemotherapy, the countless drawings he chalked up in the kitchen to post online to bask in the glory of his… what? Altruism? Artistic abilities? His decision to sleep in another room to watch his Netflix series so as '*not to disturb me*' when all I wanted was to be held and soothed as the poisons worked their way through my body. What had he *actually done* to help me through all that? The question wasn't hypothetical because I already knew the answer I had hidden for so long – absolutely sweet fuck all.

Quite the light bulb moment.

Yes, I was alone, *but I always had been*. I knew then I could and would deal with anything.

Chapter 57

When You Know, You Know

I returned to Italy, resolute.

Walking into the beach house, finding overdue utility bills strategically placed on the table (for me to take care of), a cheap, lacy, nylon night-dress in one of his drawers, and the shower blocked with long hair. With a wry smile of understanding, I recalled his stubborn objection to installing a wireless security camera I had bought. Taking in all the disappointing, predictable and unimaginative details, I could feel myself caring less and less.

Discovering he had left Buddy in the kennels the entire time was a different matter; I could barely contain my anger. Unable to face me, the spineless twat remained in Rome until I forced him back with a *We need to talk* message.

I sat waiting in the kitchen that cold day in January 2022 when he turned up visibly agitated, anxiously anticipating the third degree of an interrogation. Disconcerted by my calm demeanour, he watched me with bulging eyes as I softly explained that separation proceedings were underway. Fearing my cancer had returned, he had been the very last person I considered confiding in, which told me everything I needed to know about the state of our relationship. The lump had turned out to be a harmless side effect of the vaccination, but his irrelevance in potentially devastating news was apparent.

Listening to what I had to say, he remained impassive. Eleven years together, *this time round*, six of them married, and he had nothing, nada, zilch. There was no pleading, begging or crying from me, but my poker face wasn't down to the flicking of a switch; an internal valve had slowly and creakily turned until it was shut tight, and nothing was getting in... or out. I was living in a nightmare, and to cushion the pain, my mind was detached, numb with emotional shock.

I could only stare at this cowardly excuse of a man incapable of expressing a single thought or feeling *about anything;* my stomach turned in disgust. Knowing it was pointless, I did ask who had been there while I was away, but the detailed stories he obviously invented on the spot with his fingers pulling away at the skin on his lying lips were so ludicrously embarrassing I stopped him mid-fairytale. Angry and shattered, I still had no idea why or how it all went so wrong. I only knew I had no choice, thanks to him.

My learning curve was about to rise sharply.

A very good friend I'd met while I was away instantly recognised the shell of a human being I had become and was concerned enough to call me shortly after returning.

Gently persuading me to open up on the phone, listening carefully without labelling, accusing or blaming and allowing me time to express my bewilderment at how everything had gone so wrong, I admitted my own culpability, believing there were always two sides, citing my mood swings and inability to keep calm. I couldn't stop crying as finally all the sadness I had internalised streamed out of me, having kept a lid on how I really felt, pushing down my own emotions instead of finding solutions and carrying on regardless.

Firmly and softly cutting through my desperation, she said the words I didn't know I needed someone else to say: '*It's* not *you.*' Describing familiar behaviours and traits, her own terrible experience, her suspicions, and her overriding warning to look into it, she guided me towards a world I didn't even realise had a name, feeling as though someone had unwrapped a blindfold I had been wearing for far too long.

COVERT NARCISSISM
THE ONE YOU WON'T SEE COMING.

I researched everything I could find, reading papers written by psychologists, doctors, and experts on the subject matter and disappearing down virtual rabbit holes of endless memes, websites and YouTube videos. The defining moment was realising how many others had been through exactly the same situation – there was nothing original about the behaviour patterns of these spineless perpetrators; they ALL followed a textbook set of rules – the only difference was how long. Sometimes, I found myself gripped, immersed in a text when suddenly I dropped the phone or the paper I was reading and moved away from the source shouting out in horrified recognition. The more I read, the more I hurt as the brutal realisation hurtling towards me confirmed everything had been based on lies; every aspect of our lives had been infected by a fake. Finding out and understanding was as gratifying as it was frightening: duped, conned and manipulated, the shame and humiliation hit hard.

How could I have been so stupid? Why did I let this happen?

Because I loved and trusted him.

Meanwhile, the synapses in my brain, finally liberated, were now freely pinging off left, right and centre, flashing scenes of our lives as fast as a shutter speed camera: excuses, unexplained absences, cover-ups and irrational conversations. Suddenly, I saw them for what they really were, and my skin crawled, and I felt raw because looking at our past with the correct prescription glasses was seriously ugly. Blindsiding cruelty as over and over again something said, seen or heard would bring me to a complete stop in the middle of a mundane task while I rapidly connected the dots of yet another fabrication, deceit or nasty rumour unravelling in my head to reveal the sickening truth. The anger I experienced was a white-hot fury I was barely able to suppress, a visceral need to hurt him as deeply as he had hurt me while knowing what a hopeless waste of energy it would be.

Why? Because my new, unexpected skill now shone a light, making me face the truth: narcissistic abuse only works when YOU don't know; now fully versed in his vicious and duplicitous methods, hiding in plain sight, I knew that anything at all coming from me would simply underline who he had been busy painting me as for years, without my knowledge.

Predictably he upped his game.

Unhappy with having lost his grip, he continued sowing seeds of whispered bile to all his willing listeners. Spinning whatever martyr-style rhetoric he wished, the poor victimised husband whose wife had given him no choice because she had always done what she wanted. Gone because she had money/mental issues/a drug problem/was an alcoholic/didn't like sex/was obsessed with work./ had taken his beloved dog. Then off he skulked, leaving them all to do his dirty work.

FLYING MONKEYS
THESE ARE THE SIDEKICKS AND ENABLERS, THE FRIENDS AND ACQUAINTANCES DOING THE DIRTY WORK OF THE MAIN GUY, HAPPILY PASSING AROUND FALSE INFORMATION WHICH HELPS DISCREDIT, SMEAR, OR FURTHER ABUSE YOU. THEY ARE THE ONES EATING THE POPCORN WHILE THE ACTION FILM EXPLODES, UNAWARE OR UNCARING OF SOURCE, TRUTH OR OUTCOME.

It hurt, I can't pretend it didn't, his salacious tidbits must have been extremely satisfying and the sidelong glances and whispered exchanges I frequently encountered meant I needed to keep my head down until I felt strong enough to cope.

I left the beach house, and a tiny part of my heart broke at leaving behind a place I had invested so much in. I was told I was crazy to just walk away from it, but I knew perfectly well that despite his ostensibly genuine assurances I should rent it out in order to recoup some of the money spent, I no longer trusted a single word he said.

I asked my dad what I should do, and the answer was obvious when it came: *Material things don't matter, YOU matter.*

Chapter 58

PS I Love Me

The good times don't suddenly start from the moment you are no longer together. If only.

Recognising the cause doesn't equal an overnight fix. Treating it with whatever *you* need and taking your time is how you gradually recover. Whether you are suffering from cancer, covid, a cough, or even long-term abuse, *knowing* what it is plays a big part in the battle, but it doesn't win the war. That takes treatment and time – how much and how long depends on how deep or severe the root of the problem is.

This was not some ordinary break-up, misunderstanding or sad failure in communication. This was full-on psychological abuse, sustained and deliberate, and as a result of it happening slowly and insidiously over years, the trauma wasn't just deep, it was ingrained.

Eventually allowing myself to open up the emotional floodgates and stop pretending I was fine, I went through every stage of anger, sadness and mourning for the person I used to be and for the lie of a life I believed I'd loved, but most of all, profound grief for the devastating amount of time stolen.

I cried a lot, I shouted more.

It took time to build a new me, and it is ongoing. I am learning to accept and like what I am becoming.

Discovering what you will and won't put up with is interesting and heartbreaking. I have since learnt that personal boundaries aren't everyone's cup of tea, especially when you had none in place before. I lost many people along the way, making me question whether I really had them to start with—a painful lesson to learn, especially at my age. The circle of people I trust now maybe smaller, but they are gold.

My good times are genuinely phenomenal, exciting and adventurous, with in-between ridiculously silly stuff making me smile out loud, such as the T-shirt I found online with a crap seventies logo I then proudly wore nonstop, or being at the supermarket and flinging exactly what I want to eat and drink into the trolley, in no particular order, or when the new boxed-up arrivals of yet another house plant order arrive, and I do a happy, welcome dance around them. The joy of the spur-of-the-moment trips or the meticulously planned journeys to destinations I have longed to visit. Simply saying yes to a friend, I *will* see that concert, meet you in that airport, every single thing I do reminds me of the freedom I have regained, and it is wonderful.

I feel better, stronger, happier, and more secure every day, learning to love life again.

Every so often, something stops me in my tracks, making my stomach muscles clench as a memory or a conversation floats into my mind uninvited, like a radio channel which has inadvertently tuned in to the wrong frequency or station, a scratchy unwelcome white noise with instructions or demands. I am so much better at twisting the dial back to the peace I love and turning that channel off.

No one wants to listen to that.

Epilogue

Spring 2024

Holding a mug of tea, I stand on my terrace, taking in the overwhelming garden tasks all vying for first place on my list. I nod apologetically to the long thin branches of bougainvillea waving wildly around in the wind. If it was true that dogs and owners end up resembling each other, maybe the same is true of a garden. Those long, rebellious strands had far more in common with my own unruly hair than the rest of the obedient hedge.

I looked towards the spot where I had buried Buddy and the new tree planted above him so he'd always have shade. Waving me out of my momentary sadness, the burgeoning blossoms on the various trees around distracted me with their promises of an abundance of plums, figs, pears, apricots, and almonds, all to be made into preserves and jams in the summer.

Walking back into my beautiful house, I thought about the three free days ahead and the urgent garden list and smiled to myself.

I could start with whatever I liked, whenever I wanted, and however I pleased.

Acknowledgments

I was asked over and over again during this writing process: *What happens next? What is the next stage?* Never having written a book, I had no clue, so my standard response became, '*No idea, but I will find a way, I will make it happen.*' In retrospect, it is a pretty great motto for life.

But I didn't do it alone; I had a lot of help, and I really want to thank those who made it all happen. Firstly, to Katie McKay, my incredible editor, who saw a gem of something in my scrambled, angry and hurt blog. I wanted to work with her before we even met—when you know, you know. As the book developed, she had a magical way of encouraging me. Through tears (mine, not hers) and a lot of swearing (both) her patience, understanding and expertise coaxing better and better writing from me. See you for the next one, Katie.

The cover is down to Paul Hawkins, a diamond geezer, and his incredibly talented artist wife Linn Hart, who took a concept I had—a photograph of a bunch of narcissi—and turned it into a cover which still takes my breath away. Paul has put up with my endless worries and questions about self-publishing, listened to my never-ending voice messages and made the entire process effortless, mainly because he was doing all the work. We need more Pauls in the world.

Just as important are those who never let go of my hand: Rachael Collett, who refused to read the painful blog, having seen it first hand, preferring to wait till '*the book comes out*'. Sue Miller, who read through contracts offered but advised that '*knowing you*', self-publishing was the best route. She was so right because she knows me so well. Rich Lewis, for making me cry laughing with his messages (long live Plenty and the Donkey Stringer) and Ellen Yarborough, cheering me every step of the way because she understood. Friends unaware of holding me: Alice, Casper, Clair, Gus Sarah and Erica. And finally beautiful Martine Halliday, who 'saved' me and opened my eyes to a better future. Thank you.

Printed in Great Britain
by Amazon